THE COMPLETE GUIDE TO MAKING WOODEN CLOCKS

By John A. Nelson

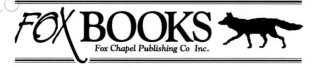

FOX BOOKS
Fox Chapel Publishing Co Inc.

1970 Broad Street
East Petersburg, PA 17520

Publisher: Alan Giagnocavo
Project Editor: Ayleen Stellhorn
Desktop Specialist: Linda L. Eberly, Eberly Designs Inc.
Interior Photography: Carl Shuman, Owl Hill Studios/Deborah Porter-Hayes
Cover Photography: Carl Shuman, Owl Hill Studios

ISBN # 1-56523-119-8

To order your copy of this book,
please send check or money order
for cover price plus $3.00 shipping to:
Fox Books
1970 Broad Street
East Petersburg, PA 17520

Manufactured in Korea

ACKNOWLEDGMENTS

Producing a comprehensive book like this requires many dedicated people. I could not have done it alone. I would like to thank the following people for their help and input: my wife Joyce, who spent hours and hours on the computer typing, struggled with my poor penmanship and put it all into a readable manuscript; Wesley and Alice Demarest of Sussex, New Jersey, for doing such an excellent job making all the clocks in this book—their woodworking skills are superior; and Debbie Porter-Hayes of Hancock, New Hampshire, for taking many of the wonderful photographs used in this book. To Alan Giagnocavo of Fox Chapel Publishing Company of East Petersburg, Pennsylvania, and his very dedicated staff: I want each of you to know how much I appreciate all your efforts. Your help and support really made this book.

The following companies supplied us with the movements and miscellaneous parts needed for each clock in this book: Armor Crafts, The American Clockmaker, Bradco Enterprises, Cherry Tree Toys, The Klockit Company, Kuempel Chime Clockworks and Studio, Merritt's Antiques, The National Artcraft Company, Precision Movements, S. LaRose Inc., The Shipley Company, The Steebar Corporation, and Turncraft Clocks Inc.

I hope you like all our efforts. Any comments or criticism, please write to me.

John A. Nelson
c/o Fox Books
1970 Broad Street
East Petersburg, PA 17520
editors@carvingworld.com

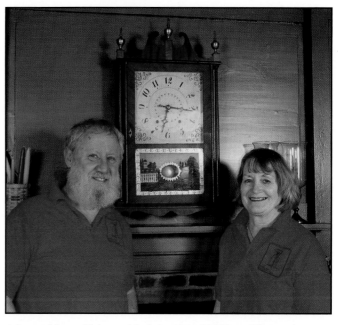

John and Joyce Nelson with their original Eli Terry Pillar and Scroll Clock.

TABLE OF

Shaker-Style Coffin Clock
page 138

CONTENTS

Three-Wood Pendulum Clock
page 65

Collector's
Shelf Clock
page 120

INTRODUCTION

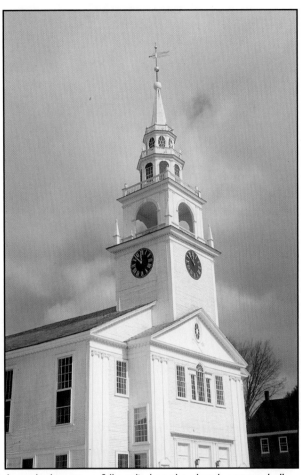

In early days, town folks relied on the church or town hall clock. Owning a clock was an indication of prosperity rather than a commitment to punctuality.

I
n years past, time passed with little or no urgency. Owning a clock was an indication of prosperity rather than a commitment to punctuality.

The passing of time has always been recognized by man, and man always had a fascination with trying to measure and record that passing. At first, it was the passing of days, the waxing and waning of the moon, and the changing of the various seasons. Time was very important in early days so that people could keep track of when to plant and harvest. The actual hour and minute of the day was not particularly important.

Early sundials were invented to keep a rough track of the passing of the hours. Other simple devices such as the hourglass, indexed candles that burned at a fixed rate and water power followed. Years later, the first mechanical clocks appeared. Today clocks of all shapes and sizes help us track time right down to the millisecond.

This book is written to appeal to anyone who likes and appreciates clocks. Various kinds of clocks and designs are included to reach all woodworking levels and all interests. I am sure there is something here for everyone. I included a little history about clocks, an introduction to the latest clock parts and accessories available today, and instructions on how to make use of them and where to get them. Noted, also, is information on the National Clock and Watch Association and a few of my favorite museums located throughout the country.

I sincerely hope you will enjoy this book and that it will get you started on a clock project of your own.

A BRIEF HISTORY OF CLOCKS

The theory behind time-keeping can be traced back to the astronomer Galileo. In 1580, Galileo, who is well-known for his theories on the universe, observed a swinging lamp suspended from a cathedral ceiling by a long chain. As he studied the swinging lamp, he discovered that each swing was equal and had a natural rate of motion. Later he found this rate of motion depended upon the length of the chain. For years he thought of this, and in 1640, he designed a clock mechanism incorporating the swing of a pendulum. Unfortunately, he died before actually building his new clock design.

In 1656, Christiaan Huygens incorporated a pendulum into a clock mechanism. He found that the new clock kept excellent time. He regulated the speed of the movement, as it is done today, by moving the pendulum bob up or down: up to "speed-up" the clock and down to "slow-down" the clock.

Christiaan's invention was the boon that set man on his quest to track time with mechanical instruments.

Early Mechanical Clocks

Early mechanical clocks, probably developed by monks from central Europe in the last half of the thirteen century, did not have pendulums. Neither did they have dials or hands. They told time only by striking a bell on the hour. These early clocks were very large and were made of heavy iron frames and gears forged by local blacksmiths. Most were placed in church belfries to make use of existing church bells.

Small domestic clocks with faces and dials started to

" Dost thou love life? Then do not squander time, for that's the stuff life is made of."

—*Benjamin Franklin*

appear by the first half of the fifteenth century. By 1630, a weight-driven lantern clock became popular in the homes of the very wealthy. These early clocks were made by local gunsmiths or locksmiths. Clocks became more accurate when the pendulum was added in 1656.

Early clock movements were mounted high above the floor on shelves because they required long pendulums and large cast-iron descending weights. These clocks were nothing more than simple mechanical works with a face and hands and were called "wags-on-the-wall." Long-case clocks, or tall-case clocks, actually evolved from the early wags-on-the-wall clocks. They were nothing more than wooden cases added to hide the unsightly weights and cast-iron pendulums.

John Harrison (1693–1776)

Little is known about this man, the one person who, I think, did the most for clock- making. John was an English clockmaker, a mechanical genius, who devoted his life to clock-making. He accomplished what Isaac Newton, known for his theories on gravity, said was impossible.

John Harrison was born March 24, 1693, in the English county of Yorkshire. John learned woodworking from his father, but taught himself how to build a clock. He made his first clock in 1713 at the age of 19. It was made almost entirely of wood with oak wheels (gears). In 1722 he constructed a tower clock for Brocklesby Park. That clock has been running continuously for over 270 years.

One year later, on July 8, 1714, England offered £20,000 (approximately 12 million dollars) to anyone whose method proved successful in measuring longitude. Such a device was desperately needed by navigators of sailing vessels. Sailors during this time were literally lost at sea as soon as they lost sight of land. One man, John Harrison, felt longitude could be measured with a clock.

During the summer of 1730, John started work on a clock that would keep precise time at sea—something no one had yet been able to do with a clock. In five years he had his first model, H-1. It weighted 75 pounds and was four feet tall, four feet wide and four feet long. To prove his theory, John built H-2, H-3 and H-4.

His method of locating longitude by time was finally

Elias Ingraham

Elias was born in 1805 in Marlborough, Connecticut. He served a 5-year apprenticeship in cabinetmaking in the early 1820s. By 1828, at the age of 23, Elias was designing and building clock cases for George Mitchell. When he was 25 years old, he worked for the Chauncey and Lawson Ives Clock Company, which was still designing and building clock cases.

Elias formed a new company with his brother Andrew in 1852 called the E. and A. Ingraham and Company, but 4 years later, it went bankrupt. A year later he formed his own company with his son, Edward. Changing the name to E. Ingraham and Company, the business began manufacturing clock cases. By 1862, his then successful company manufactured its own movements, as well.

Throughout his lifetime, Elias was granted many clock case design patents. He died in 1885, but the company he started continued. Elias was perhaps the greatest clock case designer ever, and his clock designs are still being copied and produced today.

accepted and he won the prize. It took him over 40 years. Today, his perfect timekeeper is known as a chronometer.

Clocks in the Colonies

In the early 1600s, clocks were brought to the colonies by wealthy colonists. Clocks were found only in the finest of homes. Most people of that time had to rely on the church clock on the town common for the time of day.

Most early clockmakers were not skilled in wood-working, so they turned to woodworkers to make the cases for them. These early woodworkers employed the same techniques used on furniture of the day. In 1683, immigrant William Davis claimed to be a "complete" clockmaker. He is considered to be the first clockmaker in the new colony.

Great horological artisans immigrated to the New World by 1799. Most of these early artisans settled in populous centers such as Boston, Philadelphia, New York, Charleston, Baltimore and New Haven.

Clock-making grew in all areas of the eastern part of the colonies. The earliest and most famous clockmakers from Philadelphia were Samuel Bispam, Abel Cottey and Peter Stretch. The most famous clockmaker was Philadelphia's David Rittenhouse. David succeeded Benjamin Franklin as president of the American Philosophical Society and later became Director of the United States Mint.

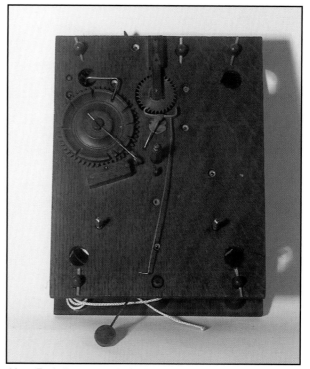

Most Early American clocks had wooden gears as brass was very expensive and hard to obtain.

Nineteenth Century Grandfather Clocks

Inexpensive tall-case clocks were made in quantity and became more affordable after 1800. The clock-making industry spread to the northeastern states. In Massachusetts, Benjamin and Ephram Willard became famous for their exceptionally beautiful long-case clocks. In Connecticut, mass-produced long-case clocks were developed by Eli Terry.

In early days, almost all clock cases were made by local cabinetmakers. A firm that specialized in clock works fashioned the wood or bronze works. Cabinetmakers engraved or painted their names on the dial faces, thereby taking claim for the completed clocks.

With the advent of the Industrial Revolution, regular

Marshall and Adams Clock Factory, Seneca Falls, New York, circa 1856.

Waterbury Clock Company

The Waterbury Clock Company started as the Benedict and Burnham Brass Manufacturing Company and, in 1850, became part of Jerome Company. With only $60,000, the Waterbury Clock Company was formed in Waterbury, Connecticut in 1857. It was a major maker of clocks in the United States from 1857 to 1944.

factory working hours and the introduction of train schedules, standardized timekeeping became a necessity. Clock-making moved to the forefront.

Wooden movements were abandoned in 1840 and 30-hour brass movements became popular. They were easy to make and inexpensive. Spring-powered movements were developed soon after. A variety of totally new and smaller clock cases appeared on the market.

Nineteenth Century Manufacturers

Clock manufacturers were mostly individual clockmakers of family-owned companies. After 1840 however, Chauncy Jerome built the largest clock factory in the United States. He started shipping clocks all over the world. The Jerome Clock Company motivated the organization of the Ansonia Clock Company and the Waterbury Clock Company. These three companies, along with Seth Thomas Company, the E. N. Welch Company, the Ingraham Clock Company, and the Gilbert Clock Company, became the major producers of clocks in the nineteenth century. There were over 30 clock factories in this country by 1851. From 1840 up to 1890, millions of clocks were produced in this country, but unfortunately, very few still exist intact today.

Clock-Making in the Twentieth Century

Most of the clockmakers who produced thousands of clocks during the 1800s failed in the twentieth century. During the stock market crash of 1929, the Ansonia Clock Company moved its operation to Russia, and the Seth Thomas Clock Company became a part of the General Time Instrument Company. From 1940 to the present, the Sessions Clock Company and the New Haven Clock Company were founded. Of the original giants of the clock industry, only three exist today: Seth Thomas is now a division of Talley Industries, the Ingraham Clock Company is now a division of McGraw-Edison, and Gilbert Clock Company has been replaced by the Sparta Corporation.

Today there are no spring-powered movements or clocks currently produced in this country. Some of the quartz movements found in today's clocks are produced here, but most are made abroad.

AMERICA'S POPULAR CLOCKS

Clock Classifications and Types

Like many antiques, clocks are classified by their overall style. There are five overall styles of clocks: Colonial, Empire, Victorian, Modern, and Contemporary.

> *Colonial* —built up to 1800; tall-case and wags-on-the-wall clocks
>
> *Empire* —1800–1840; mostly wooden movements; shelf clocks and tall-case clocks; 30-hour or 8-day movements
>
> *Victorian* —1840–1890; the period of greatest production of clocks and the greatest variety of models; advent of the 30-hour brass movement and the spring-powered movement
>
> *Modern* —1890–1940; a period of change from mechanical movements to clocks with synchronous electric motors
>
> *Contemporary* —World War II–present; great changes occur, from the development of electric motors to clocks with very accurate electronic (quartz) movements

Clocks are further categorized by types. There are three primary types of clocks: tall-case, wall and shelf.

Tall Clocks

The grandfather clock, once called the long clock, tall-case clock or even coffin clock, has always been par-

A grandfather clock kit from the American Clock Company, Model 1306E32. (Photo used with permission of the American Clock Company)

ticularly popular. The term "grandfather clock" came from a song of the same name written by Henry Clay in 1876.

The original tall-case clock is said to have been developed in London around 1650. The earliest tall-case clock built in America was made by Abel Cottey around 1720. Under the direction of Connecticut clockmaker Eli Terry, the tall-case clock was also the first household piece to be successfully mass-produced in America. Through the years, it has been known as an excellent timekeeper.

In early America, most grandfather clocks were made with flat tops. By 1740, however, during the Queen Anne period, clocks were made with round tops. The Chippendale style then became popular, followed by the most popular design, the Federal "swan-neck" top. These cases reflected the styles of the period. Other styles included Sheraton and Hepplewhite.

As glass was very expensive in those days, the front doors on grandfather clocks were made from solid wood. The solid door also hid the 42-inch-long pendulum and cast-iron weights, which were very crudely constructed.

Tall-case clock cases consist of the base, waist and hood. Some original designs included feet, waist and door columns, hood fretwork and finials. Cases were constructed from many kinds of woods, although local hardwoods such as maple, cherry, walnut and mahogany were common. Other, lower-cost clocks were made of pine. A painted grain was added to simulate the more desired and more expensive hardwood.

Many cases were very elegant and beautiful; others were extremely crude. At the height of their popularity, many tall-case clocks were over nine feet tall. Today, most range from six feet to seven feet, six inches in height. Cases shorter than six feet are considered grandmother clocks.

Wall Clocks

The wall clock was the first truly American clock made in the colonies. The most popular of all wall clocks was the small-case, elegant hanging timepiece called the "patent time-piece." Later, it was called the

William Gilbert

William Gilbert was born in 1806 and died at the age of 84 in 1890. He purchased a clock-shop with his brother-in-law, George Marsh in 1828. They made cheap clocks in Bristol, Connecticut, up to 1834. The company dissolved in 1837, but in 1841, William purchased another factory and began making clocks again. George B. Owens served as manager for over 20 years. Owens was responsible for many of the clock case designs of the W. L. Gilbert and Company.

banjo clock. It was made by Simon Willard of Massachusetts in the 1820s, and it satisfied the American fantasies of luxury and refinement of the day.

Craftsman from New Hampshire and Connecticut added a looking glass to the wall clock, thereby adding another function to the wall clock. Aaron Willard and Joseph Ives were the first clockmakers to produce many mirrored wall clocks.

Shelf Clocks

The Willards of Massachusetts designed and built the very famous first Massachusetts shelf clocks. They were usually made to order and very expensive. Affordable shelf clocks came into existence after 1807. Eli Terry received an order to build 4,000 wooden-geared movements. It took him over two years to complete the order, but his experiments helped him develop the first true mass-production factory and made shelf clocks available to everyone. The most fashionable wall clocks were replaced by cheaper shelf clocks in 1850 or so.

Major Milestones In American Clock-Making

Clock-making in America can be traced back to just prior to the American Revolution. Over the past two hundred years, various styles of clocks have become popular. These clocks were replaced by other styles as years past.

Pillar and Scroll Clock

Eli Terry is referred to as the father of American clock manufacturing. He was born in 1772, in South Windsor, Connecticut, just before the American Revolution.

In 1814, Terry developed what I feel is the most beautiful shelf clock ever built and manufactured in the United States. It was the very popular pillar and scroll shelf clock.

The original pillar and scroll varied slightly in design from 1814 to 1822. There were five slightly different wooden movements used during that time, also.

Early Eli Terry Pillar and Scroll Clock, circa 1830. Note the reverse painting on the lower section of glass. The colors were laid down in reverse order on the back of the glass.

Most of the original pillar and scroll clocks made were powered by 30-hour weight-driven, key-wound, wooden geared movements. A very few had the new improved 8-day wooden movements.

The one photographed is one of the original designs. It was made about 1820 by Eli Terry and Sons of Plymouth, Connecticut, and has a 30-hour, weight-driven, wooden movement. This clock also has an original paper that gives running instructions and the maker's name and address.

For years, many other clock companies copied the pillar and scroll clock design. Today, originals of these clocks are very expensive.

Chauncy Jerome, a carpenter working for Eli Terry at the time, is the person who actually made the first pillar and scroll clock case, although Eli Terry has always been credited with the clock.

Column and Splat Clock

In 1828, George Mitchell hired a cabinetmaker by the name of Elias Ingraham to develop a case design in order to compete with the pillar and scroll clock. Within a year, Elias created the column and splat clock. This new clock design featured columns, lion's-paw feet and a patriotic eagle splat top. (The term "splat" refers to the decorator piece at the top of the clock case.) A painting on the door glass was done with a technique called reverse painting. The painting was actually done on the inside of the glass door. Colors were laid down in a reverse order so that the painting appeared normal when viewed from the opposite side of the glass.

The column and splat clock was copied by many clockmakers of the day. To save money, some companies added a looking glass in the door in place of the reverse painting. Eli Terry developed a model of his own that he called the "transitional model," but his version was based on his original pillar and scroll design.

In time, the pillar and scroll clock was replaced by the newer clock design. Column and splat clocks were very popular from 1829 to 1845, and there were over nineteen clockmakers producing this model.

Early column and splat clock, circa 1840. The "splat" is the top trim piece.

Column Clock

During the Victorian period, the new popular clock was the column clock. Note the classical influence and empire base and gilded columns. These column clocks were made in Connecticut, New York and Massachusetts as early as 1824 and as late as 1885. They reflect the formal styles of popular furniture of the day. Column clocks were made with two or even three doors and some had both a looking glass and reversed painting.

Column clocks were more expensive than other shelf clocks of the day. Some of them had the somewhat new and improved 8-day, spring-driven brass movements.

These clocks usually had white-painted-tin dial faces. Some had openings in the center of the dial faces so the brass movements could be seen. This also allowed the oiling of the verge and escapement wheel.

Ogee Clock

There is something about the ogee clock that everyone likes. Many clock collectors started their collections with an ogee. I once went to an auction and watched one person buy five of them. He wasn't a collector or dealer—he simply liked them!

The ogee name is derived from the name of the simple, curved molding used in the clock's construction. This clock is nothing more than a rectangular box with a door with an ogee molding. It has simple, weight-driven brass works that just about anyone can take apart and repair. It is among the simplest of clocks made.

These simple clocks were made as early as 1827. It is not know who designed the ogee clock, though many speculate it was Chauncey Jerome. They were moderately priced clocks and were popular from 1830 to 1859.

The very first ogee clocks had wooden geared movements, but overall, most had simple 30-hour, weight-driven brass movements. Some ogee clocks had a mirror in the door; more expensive models had reversed paintings on the door. Ogee clocks came in all sizes, from the very small (4 inches deep, 11^1/$_2$ inches wide and 18 inches high) to the very large model (5^1/$_2$ inches

Column clock from the Victorian period, circa 1875.

Simple ogee clock with mirrored door.

Calendar clocks provided the hour of the day, day of the week, day of the month and month of the year.

A popular Gothic design is the steeple clock.

deep, 18 inches wide and 31 inches high). The ogee on page nine is a standard size (4¹/₂ inches deep, 15¹/₂ inches wide and 25 ³/₄ inches high).

Some ogee clocks have a flat molding in place of the ogee molding and are referred to as "beveled-case clocks" or "flat ogee clocks."

Calendar Clock

Clockmakers developed a timepiece in 1850 that provided the hour of the day, day of the week, day of the month, and month of the year. Some models even indicated the phase of the moon, as well as high and low tides. Every 24 hours, at midnight, a pin on a gear turned once, putting the calendar mechanism into operation. Calendar clocks were adapted into the schoolhouse clock style.

The calendar clock gave its owner a method of long-range planning. We rely today on desk calendars, quartz watches, electric clocks, radios or television. Remember, in 1870 and before the adoption of standard time, this calendar information was not readily available to everyone.

The Ithaca Clock Company, the Ansonia Brass and Copper Company and the Waterbury Clock Company started making their own calendar clocks in 1880. These calendar clocks were very popular until 1910. Today, calendar clocks are sought after by almost all clock collectors.

This model at the upper left was manufactured by Seth Thomas and patented on December 18, 1875. It is a pedimented, partial-octagon clock in the Victorian style with some Gothic influence. This model counts the hours, on the hour, and rings once every half hour.

Steeple Clock

The Connecticut clockmaker, Elias Ingraham, who designed the column and splat clock, was also a skilled cabinetmaker. He designed and produced many fine clock cases of the day.

In 1845, he designed an unusual "sharp," gothic clock case that featured church-like spires. Today it is called the steeple clock.

The steeple clock is one of the most popular clock models ever made. It is still being reproduced today. In its day, this clock was copied by most all existing clock companies.

Most early steeple clocks contained a 30-hour brass movement. Eight-day movement models are somewhat rare, cost much more and are more desirable. Steeple clocks range in height from 10$^1/2$ inches to 23 inches.

Cottage Clock

Cottage clocks are a simple, pleasant form of the Connecticut shelf clock. The cottage clocks were popular during the Victorian age and replaced the somewhat larger, more expensive box clocks of the day.

Cottage clocks are very small. Each clock was usually less than 12 inches high. Most models had simple 30-hour movements; some even had alarms.

Cottage clocks were made in great volume from 1865 through 1895. Many models had decorated doors.

Today, cottage clocks are still fairly popular. Unfortunately, they are of limited value because of their 30-hour movement.

Figure Eight Clock

The figure eight clock is shaped like a number eight. The top circle, which houses the clock face, is usually larger than the bottom circle. It is another early example of Elias Ingraham's work. He patented this design around 1862 and named it the "ionic" wall clock.

Elias hired Anson Atwood to set up and run a movement manufacturing division of the Ingraham Company. This allowed the company to manufacture both the movement and the case. Before this time, Elias had purchased movements from Noah Pomeroy and the Waterbury Brass Company.

The figure eight clock was the forerunner of the popular schoolhouse clock, developed in 1875 by the Ansonia Clock Company.

Cottage clocks were popular from 1865 to 1895.

The figure eight clock is the forerunner of the popular schoolhouse clock.

Banjo Clock

The Willard family of Massachusetts designed and built many beautiful clocks.

In 1795, Simon designed a totally new wall clock, which he called the "improved time-piece." He patented it in 1802, and it was an instant success with the burgeoning middle class. The case is shaped like a banjo. Famous naval battles were painted on the bottom glass ,and the top glass panel was gold-gilded with a matching design. Some banjo clocks had brass side brackets. Today, clocks built by Benjamin, Simon, Ephram and Aaron Willard demand top dollar, if you can find one for sale. Simon Willard learned clockmaking from his older brother, Benjamin, and settled in Roxbury, Massachusetts, right after the Revolutionary War.

The "improved time piece" is a Banjo clock. It was patented in 1802 by Simon Willard.

Schoolhouse Clock

For many years, schoolhouse clocks were hung on the wall next to Gilbert Stuart's framed painting of George Washington in school rooms all over the country. I hate to date myself, but I can vividly remember those days myself. Unfortunately, those wonderful old clocks have been replaced today by "cold" high-tech electronic clocks.

In 1875, the Ansonia Clock Company developed a very popular clock, the Model-A long drop octagon clock—a forerunner of the schoolhouse clock. This model was an instant success and was sold throughout the entire world almost overnight.

The long drop octagon clock was shortened and became what we recognize as a schoolhouse clock.

Schoolhouse clocks were sold from 1875 to 1910, but they didn't go out of style until the 1950s. The clocks were eventually made in all sizes by almost all major clock companies. Countries such as China and Korea also made schoolhouse clocks in great quantities. Today many of the so-called antique schoolhouse clocks you find in antique shops are actually Korean, not American antiques. Care should be taken in buying an old school house clock.

The Ansonia Clock Company made excellent, high-quality movements, but due to the Great Depression, it

Schoolhouse clocks were popular from 1875 to 1910.

went out of business in 1929. What was left of the company was moved to Russia, but it never really regained the success it had achieved in the United States.

Regulator Clock

The term "Regulator" generally refers to a very precise, plain-cased clock with a long pendulum and no bell chimes to sound the hour. Seth Thomas' original and famous Regulator No. 2 wall clock was very popular in America from 1870 to 1920. Almost every office, church or bank of any size at all had a Regulator No. 2 hanging on the wall.

Regulator No. 2 was made of oak (sometimes walnut), with an 8-day, high-quality, weight-driven movement. The movement was mounted on a heavy cast-iron support, which is a little unusual for most American clocks. The design changed very little throughout all the years of manufacturing. An exact copy of this movement with the cast-iron support can be still purchased today.

Gingerbread Clock

The most common and, until recently, the least liked clock from the Victorian age is the gingerbread clock. When first introduced in 1800, it was called the "Kitchen Clock." The gingerbread clock was very popular in the Victorian homes of the middle and lower classes. They were in vogue until 1900. Later models used pressed molded wings and tops. These were stamped out of wood by the tens of thousands. Gingerbread clocks were made in all shapes and sizes—most not very attractive at all. These clocks were made of oak or walnut. Today, original gingerbread clocks are gaining in popularity again, and their cost is rising yearly.

Gingerbread clocks had striking movements on a bell for each hour and single strikes for the half hour. An accessory was an obnoxious alarm that would drive you out of bed very quickly—like it or not!

I think the only elegant gingerbread clock ever made was the Patti Parlor walnut model. It was manufactured by G.N. Welch Manufacturing Company in 1887, and today it is sought after by many clock collectors.

Regulator Clock No. 2 was one of America's favorite office clocks. Popular from 1870 to 1920, most were made of oak, but a few were made of walnut.

A clock design from the Victorian age is the gingerbread clock. Most were made of oak.

Mission clocks replaced the gingerbread clocks.

Mission Clock

The Mission clocks were developed at the end of the Victorian era and replaced the gingerbread models. They were an effort to return to a simple and honest design and were popular from 1900 until 1930.

Mission clocks were usually made of oak, as was most Mission furniture of the time. The clocks were made to convey the functionalist designers' sense of moral commitment or "mission" to create a simple and pure design. They were made as tall-case clocks, wall clocks and mantel clocks.

Black Mantel Clock

American clock companies developed a totally new small black mantel clock in 1870. These clocks were well-made and inexpensive; they were manufactured using the latest clock technology of the day and had all the new and improved features.

Black mantel clocks were nothing more than a rectangular, wooden, black-painted box with either Doric

Dates of Operation for Major American Clock Manufacturers

E. Ingraham & Co.
1861-1958

Elias Ingraham & Co.
1857-1860

E.N. Welch Mfg. Co.
1864-1903

F. Kroeber (& Co.)
1863-1887

F. Kroeber Clock Co.
1887-1904

Gilbert Mfg. Co.
1866-1871

New Haven Clock Co.
1853-c.-1965

Sessions Clock Co.
1903-1956

Seth Thomas
1813-1853

Seth Thomas Clock Co.
(Plymouth Hollow, CT)
1853-1865

Seth Thomas Clock Co.
(Thomaston, CT)
1866-1930

Seth Thomas Div. Of
General Time
1930-present

Waterbury Clock Co.
1857-1944

William L. Gilbert Clock Co.
1871-1934

William L. Gilbert
Clock Corp.
1934-1957

W.L. Gilbert & Co.
1845-1848, and 1851-1866

or Ionic columns. Many of these clocks have lion heads mounted on the sides and brass, claw-like feet on the bottom.

Real marble was incorporated into the design of some of the black mantel clocks during the Victorian era. Most clockmakers, used a painted marble veneer, called admantine, over wood. Black mantel clocks were popular for over 40 years, from 1880 to 1920, but were eventually replaced by the new model Tambour clock.

William Gilbert Welch, along with all major clock manufacturing companies of the day, made black mantel clocks in very large quantities. They were made in all kinds of shapes and sizes, with all kinds of column combinations and decorations. Today you can still find many of these clocks in antique shops throughout the country. Some are very pretty; many were not pretty at all.

Until recently, black mantel clocks were not very popular, but today they are gaining more and more interest from collectors. Their movements are of the highest quality of the day, keep excellent time, and will run for another 100 years or more. These black clocks are the "sleepers" of the antique world. I feel in a few years they will be in demand and their prices will increase dramatically.

Black mantel clocks were well made and used excellent, dependable movements.

Tambour Clock

The Tambour clock replaced the black mantel clocks around 1908. Tambour clocks are sometimes referred to as "humpback" clocks. They had their heyday from 1920 to 1930 but were still popular up to 1950. The clock is shaped like a tambourine drum, hence the name "Tambour." These clocks are not antiques as most of them are not over one hundred years old, yet.

Experts estimate that over a million Tambour clocks have been made. Most contain either an 8-day or 30-day movement. Today they are referred to simply as mantel clocks and are still being made, though most Tambour clocks manufactured today incorporate the new quartz movement.

The Tambour clock is sometimes called the "Humpback" clock. They had their heyday from 1920 to 1930. They were the last mass-produced clock and the last clock with mechanical movements made in this country.

Conclusion

Many clocks of foreign design, including the Vienna wall clock and the Black Forest cuckoo clock, have also been popular in America. Some are produced here in the United States. However, the Tambour clock is really the last vastly popular American model to be developed. No other clock model has since been produced to take its place in the United States.

A Vienna Regulator clock made from Kit No. 1340W42 sold by the American Clock Co. (Photo used with permission of the American Clock Co.)

A Cuckoo clock made from Kit No. 6342010 from the American Clock Co. (Photo used with permission of the American Clock Co.)

CLOCK COMPONENTS

If you spend a lot of time making a clock—and you will—you do not want to skimp and use inexpensive, poorly made components. Today, there are all kinds of clock-related components available. These wonderful components add that "finished," professional look. The suppliers listed in the appendix have high-quality components. A few of their products are illustrated here to give you an idea of some of the components that are available.

Ordering Parts

Parts vary slightly from vendor to vendor. A six-inch-diameter dial face from one vendor might measure 6¹/₄ inches in diameter from another vendor. It is important that you order the hardware and movement before starting a clock project so that you can make minor adjustments for slight differences in purchased parts. Also check that the movement's dimensions are correct. If a pendulum is used, check that the pendulum length is correct and that it will swing properly in the given space. Check that the length of the center hand shaft is long enough, but not too long, as the tip of the center hand shaft must not touch the glass on the dial face (if glass is used).

If you use a quartz movement you should not have any problems at all, except for the length of the center shaft. Unlike a spring-powered movement, the pendulum length on a quartz movement has no effect on the operation of the movement like a spring-powered movement does, so the pendulum can be cut to any length as necessary.

The brass dial bezel diameter also has a tendency to vary slightly from vendor to vendor, so you should check these as well before starting a project. If possible, try to get dial face bezels with the glass and dial already assembled.

Choosing a Clock Movement

Quartz movements are rather simple to install and instructions are usually included. The mechanical brass movements usually do not include instructions, so you should have a basic knowledge of how to adjust and set up these movements.

Whether purchasing a quartz or mechanical movement, you must consider the following:

Price: Avoid the least expensive movements.

Length of center shaft: Quartz movements are usually attached to the dial face through the center hole. Be sure to double-check this length.

Note: Because the quartz movement is attached through the dial face, you must purchase a movement with the correct center shaft length. A thin dial requires a short center shaft. A thick dial requires a long center shaft. Allow enough length for the nut and washer. Be sure the center shaft is not too long so that it hits the glass door (if used).

Pendulum length: The pendulum (if one is required) does not make the quartz movement run; it is for appearance only. The length of the pendulum is usually considered the length from the center of the dial to the center of the pendulum bob, though sometimes it is measured from the center of the dial to the tip of the pendulum bob. Watch that the pendulum does not hit the sides of the case.

Chimes: Check that space is available to accommodate chimes if they are required.

Size of movement: Make sure the size of the movement is appropriate for the space available.

Important: It is a good idea to order the movement before beginning work on the clock so you can recheck its fit as you make the case. The movements listed in the parts list are only suggestions; many companies sell similar movements or parts. You should stay with the correct pendulum length and use the correct hand style, if possible.

Today, quartz movements come in all shapes and sizes. They can easily be adapted to replace most any original movement. Although they are not authentic, they do keep excellent time, do not require weekly winding, and run very quietly. Quartz movements can be ordered with or without pendulums. They come with bells, chimes, and bim-bam chimes.

The best way to cut holes for quartz inserts is to use a Forstner bit. Forstner bits come in all sizes. You must, however, use a drill press to make use of these bits.

The Clock Face

The clock face is the most important part of the clock. This is what you notice first, and of course, the part you look at to tell the time. The dial, the hands and the bezel should match the overall style of the clock. This is important. For example, Victorian-style numbers or fancy hands would look out of place on an ultra-modern clock.

Dials: Original dials were made of paper, wood, zinc, brass and iron.

The dial's size is considered the diameter of the minute hand's track.

If you purchase a dial, you have the following choices:

Style of numbers: Arabic or Roman
Diameter of the minute track
Ornamentation of the corners
Type of material: paper, wood, zinc, etc.
Approximate size of the numbers
Color: white, off white, etc.
Finish: gloss or dull
Specific shape and size

Hands: Clock hands come in a great variety of styles and sizes. It is important to order hand sizes that will fit the minute track. The minute hand should be the same size or slightly smaller than the radius of the minute track of the dial.

For example, if the distance from 9 o'clock to 3 o'clock is six inches (dial diameter), then the correct hand length would be three inches or less. Also, the second hand should be equal to or less than the length of the minute hand.

On quartz movements, the hour hand is simply pushed on the largest diameter center shaft and the minute hand is attached to the thinner diameter center shaft. You can carefully rotate the hour hand around on the shaft to any position on the dial you wish, but the minute hand fits into a slot and is held in place with a nut. If you have a chiming movement, carefully turn the minute hand until the movement strikes. Count the strikes, rotate the small hour hand to the correct hour. Take care setting the hands and never turn the hands backwards.

Again, the style of the hands should match the style of the clock.

Bezel: The brass frame that holds the clock's dial face and glass in place is called the bezel. Be sure to purchase the movement, hands and bezel before starting any work on the case. You may have to fit them to the case.

On some clocks, the bezel and dial are one unit. These inserts are much easier to use because the glass comes with the assembly already mounted, ready for the clock case. You only need to drill a hole to fit the insert.

HAND MEASUREMENT is made from the center of the shaft hole to the tip of the hand. The minute hand length is half or less than the dial diameter.

#1
#2 2 3/4"
#3 2 1/2"
#4 2 3/8"
#5 1 3/4"
#6 1 7/16"
#7 3 5/16"

3 7/16"

#8 2 1/16"
#9 3"
#10 4 3/4"
#11 3 3/8"
#12 1 3/4"
#13 3 1/8"
#14 2 1/4"

#15 2 1/4"
#16 4 3/16"
#17 2 7/8"
#18 3 7/16"
#19 4 1/4"
#20 4 1/8"

#21 1 1/2"
#22 1 7/8"
#23 3"
#24 1 5/8"
#25 1 7/8"
#26 2 5/8"
#27 3 1/16"

STEEBAR CORP.

Grandfather Clocks

Today, large clocks such as Grandfather clocks and large wall clocks take mechanical movements very easily. The Kieninger cable-driven 9-tube movement is one of the finest large movements made and available today.

Clock Kits ▶

There are many wonderful clock kits for those who would love to build a clock but do not have all the wood-working tools to make all the pieces. These kits are a lot of fun to make. They are perfect for those who want a head start.

AMERICAN CLOCKMAKER

▼ Mechanical Movements

ARMOR CRAFTS

In years past, brass mechanical movements were always used to power clocks. Today brass mechanical movements are still available and will give you the real ticking effect. Brass movements require a lot of work to fit them into a clock, and the movements must be wound once a week or once a month, however, the effort is well worth the finished result.

Some brass movements are designed for quick and easy installation. Armor Crafts has a beautiful bim-bam chime unit that is complete and very simple to install.

Electric Movements ▼

Electric movements are also available. They are easy to install and can be used in new clocks or to repair worn electric movements in old clocks.

STEEBAR CORP.

STEEBAR CORP.

STEEBAR CORP.

STEEBAR CORP.

KLOCKIT CO.

Quartz Gear Movements

This is an example of a quartz-powered movement with gears showing. It makes a great combination of quartz power with the look of mechanical gears.

Another quartz/gear movement is the 400-day anniversary movement. You can build a clock around this movement. It even comes with a glass dome if you wish.

KLOCKIT CO.

Quartz Weight Driven Movement

Quartz weight-driven movements are also available. In a quartz movement such as this one, the weights are false but look real. You can design and build a clock around this movement.

KLOCKIT CO.

STEEBAR CORP.

PRECISION MOVEMENT

TURNCRAFT CLOCKS

CHERRY TREE

ARMOR CRAFTS

Fit-ups or Insert Movements

One of the easiest movements to use is the fit-up movement. It comes complete with movement, dial face, bezel and hands—one simple-to-use unit. You have to cut a round hole to mount these clocks.

Some fit-ups come with photos on the face, which add a lot to your clock with no extra work for you.

There are even multi-functional units available with time, day, date and moon phase all built in. These make your clock even more helpful.

Simple Quartz Movements ▶

Simple quartz movements are the most popular movements and have the most flexibility. They come with and without pendulums and with or without chimes or bells. In choosing a simple quartz movement, be sure to check the shaft length. Check how thick the dial face is and order a shaft length slightly longer than the thickness of the dial face.

Simple quartz movements can be purchased in extra-long 31-inch pendulum lengths so that they can be used in grandfather clocks.

An interesting option for a special quartz movement is a moonphase dial.

ARMOR CRAFTS

ARMOR CRAFTS

PRECISION MOVEMENT

Dial Faces ▶

If you use a simple quartz movement, a dial face and hands must be used with it. Dial faces come in plain, thick paper, brass or wood. Some come with brass bezel, hinge and glass ready to mount.

Faces come with brass trim similar to the dial faces used in regular or Vienna clocks. These give a formal flair to most any clock.

Very fancy, beautiful grandfather clock dials are also available. They come with raised corners and numbers. Some come with a moon phase dial.

PRECISION MOVEMENT

PRECISION MOVEMENT

CHERRY TREE TOYS, INC.

◀ *Brass Components*

High-quality components add a lot to any project. Heavy solid-brass hinges are a must on any quality clock project.

Brass screws always look good. Keep in mind they are soft and break very easily. It is a good idea to use a steel screw first, then remove it and add the brass screws. (I also use wax from a candle to lubricate brass screws.)

Brass hangers always add "class" to any project. Attach them with brass screws or tacks. You might want to polish the hanger before attaching it to the clock.

Antique brass corners are available for dial faces or trim pieces.

High-quality brass finials and eagles give an expensive, finished look. People will admire and appreciate these components for years to come.

◀ *Desk Accessories*

Pencil and pen sets can be used with desk clocks.

MAKING YOUR OWN CLOCK

In general, clockmaking follows the same steps. Those steps are outlined later in this chapter when we show you how to make a coffin clock.

Before You Begin

Everyone has different woodworking tools and different skill levels. Take your time and enjoy yourself when you make your clock. If you need to learn more about a tool or hone your woodworking skills in a certain area, do that before you start your clock project.

As with any woodworking project, carefully study the drawings before starting so you know exactly how the clock is assembled and how each individual part is made. Try to go through each process step-by-step in your mind so you will know how to make each part with the tools and equipment available to you. As you proceed, keep all cuts square and all tool edges sharp.

Tools

Making the clocks from the plans in this book requires very few tools. Basic hand tools will be needed, along with the following power tools:
- table saw or radial-arm saw
- router and/or shaper
- jigsaw or scroll saw
- lathe (for 1 or 2 clocks only)
- sander planer (optional, but handy)

Caution: Always utilize extreme caution when using any tool and maintain safe practices to avoid accidents. Be sure to wear eye and ear protection.

Using the Drawings

Any information specific to the 37 clock projects in this book is noted with the plans for that particular project.

Two or three views are provided for each clock project: a **front view,** a **right side view** and/or a **top view.**

The front view is always the most important view and should be your starting point. As space allows, the right-side view is located directly to the right of the front view; the top view is located directly above the front view. All features in the front view are transferred directly to the right-side view and the top view.

Dashed lines on the drawing indicate a hidden surface of a feature within the object. Think of these hidden lines as X-rays showing what the inside of the clock looks like.

A thin line made up of short and long dashes is the **centerline** (C/L). It indicates the exact center of the clock or part.

Important: All drawings are fully dimensioned. The actual required size is called-off and is the distance between the tips of the arrowheads.

Section views are sometimes used to further illustrate a particular feature of the clock, to illustrate how an area is assembled, or to show the shape or profile of a molding. On the drawing, two arrows are drawn with an A or a B at the tips of the arrows. The section view shows what the piece would look like if the clock were cut in two at the arrows. This view will be listed as "View at A–A" or

"View at B–B."

Study the drawings very carefully. Some parts must be made in a right-hand and left-hand pair. The side of a clock is a good example: Both sides of the clock are the same, but you must make a right side and a left side.

In addition to the regular views, most projects have an **exploded view** that illustrates how the clock parts fit together. Again, be sure you fully understand how the clock is assembled before you start any work.

Parts List

Most clocks have a complete parts list specifying every part used in the clock. On the parts list, the number to the left of the part is the same number noted on the drawing. Each part can be easily found and copied by matching the numbers.

Important: All efforts have been made to ensure that the dimensions of each part are correct; however, it is always best to recheck each part with its mate by dry-fitting all of the parts as you proceed.

Materials

A clock is the focal point of any room. In addition to being a functional object, a clock is also a decoration.

Wes and Alice Demarest, who cut the clocks featured in this book, went out of their way to use different kinds of wood and various combinations to illustrate what unique and unusual woods look like on the project clocks. (See Appendix B.) It doesn't take any more time to make a project out of a plain piece of pine than it does to make it from an interesting piece of purpleheart or zebra wood.

The cost of using an unusual wood is a little more—in fact it could be five times more—but most projects in this book do not use very much material, so the actual cost is not excessive. Your decision to choose an unusual, highly grained, interesting wood will guarantee that your clock will be admired for years to come.

Adhesives

We used Titebond® wood glue for both hardwood and softwood clocks in this book. The surfaces need to be clean and dry in order for the adhesive to work properly. Dry fit all the pieces and trim them if necessary before gluing; joints should fit snugly. To ensure a good bond, spread the glue and clamp the pieces in place for thirty minutes or more. Let the glue dry for another twenty-four hours. Be sure not to get glue on the wood surfaces.

For glass, plastic or metal use a product called E-6000®. This is an adhesive used in industry and is an exceptional craft adhesive for all kinds of applications. Apply E-6000® to both surfaces. Allow the pieces to bond for ten minutes or so, then press the surfaces together. Let the pieces dry for five or six hours before handling. A 48-hour period is required for E-6000® to dry to full strength.

Finishing Instructions

After completing your clock, you are now ready to finish it. This is the most important part of clockmaking and should not be rushed. Remember, the clock you make will be seen for years to come. Beautiful wood, good hardware and perfect joints can not overcome a poor finish; that alone will ruin your project.

Preparing

Before applying any stain, you must first prepare the wood. The following preliminaries are imperative to a quality finish.

• All joints should be checked for tight fits. If necessary, apply water putty to all joints, allowing ample time for drying. Set and fill nail heads with water putty.

• Sand the clock all over in the direction of the wood grain. If you are sanding by hand, use a sanding block and keep all of the clock's corners sharp. Sand all over using 100-grit paper. Resand with 120-grit paper. If necessary, sand a final time with 180-grit paper. Take care not to round the edges.

• If you do need or want any of the edges rounded, use 120-grit paper, then 180-grit paper to round the edges.

• Carefully check that all surfaces are smooth, dry and dust-free before proceeding.

Staining

There are two major kinds of stain: water stains and oil stains.

Water stains are purchased in powder form and mixed as needed by dissolving the powder in hot water. Water stains have a tendency to raise the grain of the wood. If you use a water stain, sand the clock lightly with fine paper after the stain dries.

Oil stains are made from pigments ground in linseed oil. They do not raise the grain.

Before you begin, test the stain on a scrap piece of the same kind of lumber you plan to use to make certain you have the correct color.

When applying stain, wipe or brush on the stain as quickly and as evenly as possible to avoid overlapping streaks. If you want a darker finish, apply more than one coat of stain. Try not to apply too much stain on the end grain.

Allow the piece to dry in a dust-free area for at least 24 hours.

Fillers

Use a paste filler for porous wood such as oak or mahogany to ensure a smooth finish. Purchase paste filler slightly darker than the color of the wood; the wood you use will darken with age.

Before using paste filler, thin it with turpentine so it can be applied with a brush. Use a stiff brush and work in the direction of the grain to fill the pores. After 15 or 20 minutes, wipe off the excess with a piece of burlap pulled gently across the grain. Take care to leave filler in the pores. Let the filler dry for 24 hours. Apply a second coat if necessary.

Finishes

Shellac is a hard finish that is easy to apply and dries in a few hours. For best results, thin the shellac slightly with alcohol and apply an extra coat or two. Several coats of thin shellac are much better than one or two thick coats. Sand the piece lightly with extra-fine sand paper between coats, then rub the entire surface with a dampened cloth.

Varnish is easy to brush on and dries to a smooth, hard finish within 24 hours. It makes an excellent finish that is transparent and gives a deep-finish look to your project. Be sure to apply varnish in a completely dust-free area. Apply one or two coats directly from the can with long even strokes. Rub between each coat. After the last coat, rub with 0000 steel wool.

Oil finishes are especially easy to use for the clock projects in this book. They are easy to apply, long lasting, never need sanding and actually improve the wood permanently. Apply a heavy, wet coat uniformly to all surfaces and let the finish dry for 20 or 30 minutes. Wipe the clock completely dry until you have a nice, satin finish.

Paint

Five projects in this book require paint. The painted surface of these projects should look smooth with no hint of grain or a "wood look."

To achieve a smooth, painted finish, apply three or four coats of primer paint, sanding between each coat of paint. Apply at least two coats of paint. Sand between coats. After the last coat of paint, rub with #0000 steel wool. This will make the surface very smooth, but slightly dull. Apply a final coat of butcher wax to bring back the shine. This will give you a beautiful, satin-rich finish. Take care not to rub the paint off at the edges of the wood or molding.

Step-by-Step
Making a Coffin Clock

Our goal in this demonstration is to show you the basic steps that go into making your own clock. We chose the coffin clock because it is a classic clock with simple lines. It also incorporates an "all-in-one" dial and bezel and a quartz movement. The complete plans for making the Shaker-Style Coffin Clock and a photograph of the finished clock are found on pages 138–140.

1 Plane the wood to the correct thickness. Each board will be planed to the thickness given in the parts list on page 138. Planing can also be done by hand.

2 Sand the top and bottom surfaces.

3 Make a 1/4" wide by 1/4" deep rabbet in the two side pieces (part no. 1).

4 Locate and cut the 7 1/2" diameter hole for the dial face in the front door (part no. 2).

5 Locate and cut the 1³/₄" by 2³/₄" oval in the front door (part no. 2).

6 Make the two ⁵/₈" wide by ⁵/₁₆" deep rabbets in the door (part no. 2).

7 Sand the inside edges of the hole for the dial face and the pendulum hole.

8 Using a router bit with a ball-bearing follower, make a rabbet ¹/₄" deep and ⁵/₁₆" wide to hold the glass in place.

9 Using a ¹/₄" radius bit with a ball-bearing follower, give the two holes on the front door rounded edges.

10 Glue and screw the back (part no. 3) to the two sides (part no. 1). Keep everything at 90 degrees.

11 Locate and add the two dial supports (part no. 7). Glue and screw in place.

12 Layout and make the top splat (part no. 5). Sand all over.

14 Locate and make two notches for the hinges on the right side of the clock case.

13 Glue up the top (part no. 4), the splat (part no. 5) and the two braces (part no. 6) as shown on the plans. The final assembly should look like this.

15 Attach the dial face to the backing board (part no. 8) with spray adhesive. Check to make sure it is the center of the opening.

16 Attach the movement and the hands.

17 Screw the dial face and backing board in place so that the face appears in the center of the door hole cut out.

18 Attach the door. Check that it lines up correctly.

19 Attach the top and bottom (part no. 4) to the sides and back. Screw in place. Do not use any glue.

20 Add the latch and screw as shown.

21 Add the glass to the door (in the cut out sections) using black putty).

22 Add the long pendulum. You may have to add an extension to the rod so that the bob can be seen in the center of the little oval window.

CAT LOVER'S WALL CLOCK

Special instructions

- Use a photocopier to enlarge the plans 165%.
- Choose an interesting piece of wood $3/4"$ x $9^{1}/4"$ x $14^{1}/4"$.
- Add a hanger and a $2^{5}/16"$-diameter insert.
- Insert $2^{5}/16"$-dia. National Artcraft No. 179-062-07

Cats are always popular. If you like cats, this simple wall clock is just for you. Of course, it will also make a great gift for cat lovers. Our sample was made of red elm. If you can find it, use $7/8$-inch-thick wood.

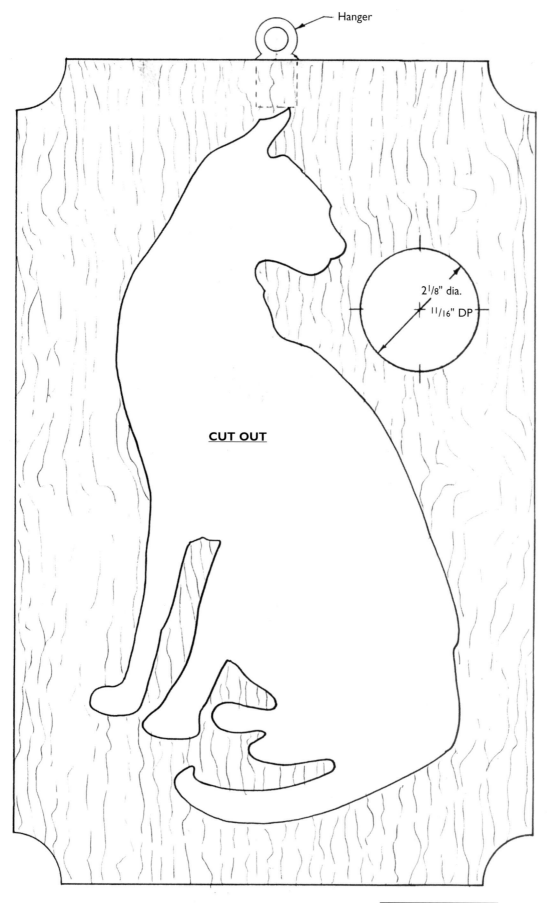

Hanger

2 1/8" dia.
11/16" DP

CUT OUT

Enlarge 165%

INSERT: KLOCKIT CO.

This clock will make a great project for those in the family who love wildlife. It is a simple one-piece plaque-style clock. You might want to add a mirrored piece of Plexiglas behind the cut-out pattern to really enhance the clock.

Special instructions

- Use a photocopier to enlarge the plans 130%.
- Choose a nice piece of wood $^1/_2$" x $8^1/_2$" x 9".
- Use a 1 $^3/_8$" diameter Forstner bit to drill a $^1/_4$" deep hole for the movement.
- Add a 2" diameter insert.
- Add a Plexiglas® mirror (optional).

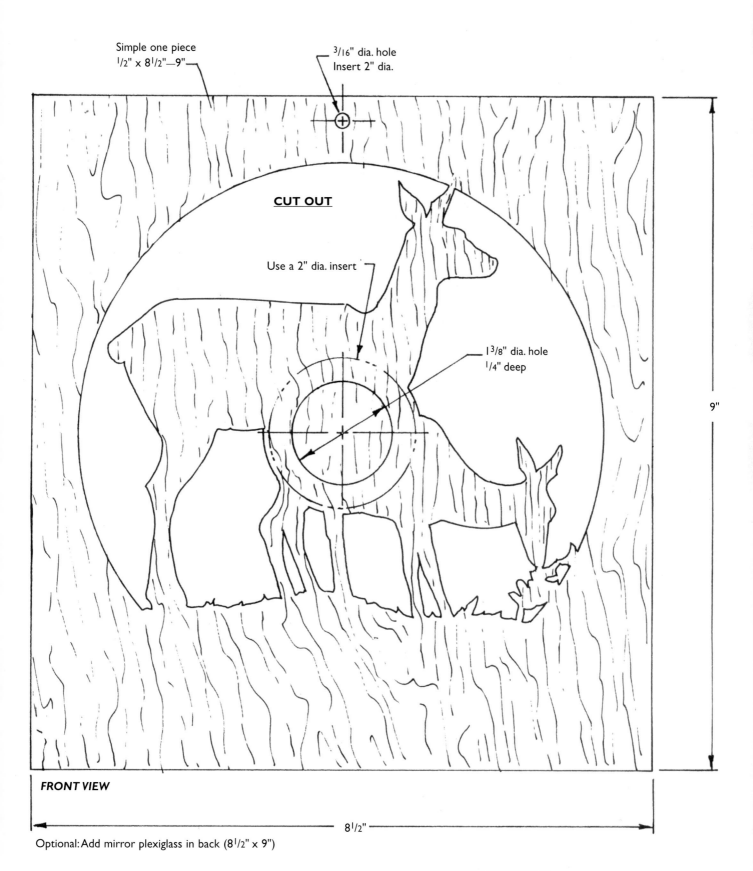

Simple one piece
$^1/2$" x $8^1/2$"—9"

$^3/16$" dia. hole
Insert 2" dia.

CUT OUT

Use a 2" dia. insert

$1^3/8$" dia. hole
$^1/4$" deep

9"

FRONT VIEW

$8^1/2$"

Optional: Add mirror plexiglass in back ($8^1/2$" x 9")

Enlarge 130%

This is a simple clock style for your desk. This contemporary model uses a $1^7/16$ diameter clock insert. A more traditional style desk clock is shown in the next project.

2"

³/₄"

⁵/₁₆" DP

1³/₈" dia.

2⁷/₈"

¹/₂"

2³/₄"

1¹/₈"

FRONT VIEW

SIDE VIEW

Special instructions

- Use the plans at full size. Choose a nice hardwood and cut pieces to overall size. Locate and drill a 1³/₈-inch-diameter hole, ⁵/₁₆ deep for the insert.
- Carefully glue the top section to the base as shown—take care not to let glue squeeze out over the base.
- Add four ¹/₂-inch-diameter felt pad feet (not shown).
- Use a 1⁷/₁₆" dia. mini insert (Merritt's Antiques P-1273).

³/₄" × 2" – 2⁷/₈"

¹/₂" × 1¹/₈" – 2³/₄"

PICTORIAL VIEW

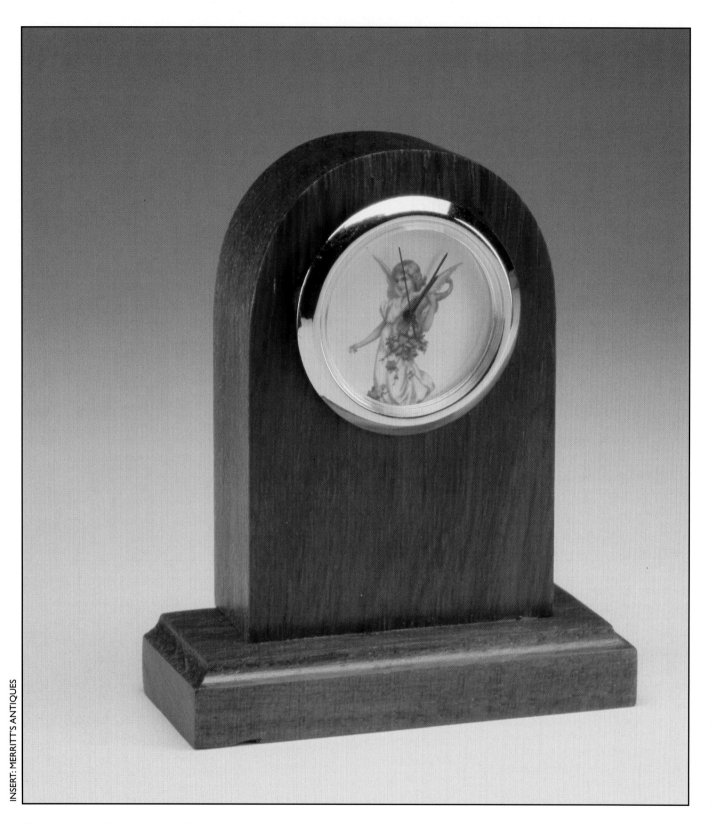

INSERT: MERRITT'S ANTIQUES

This is a simple clock style for your desk. It is very similar to the clock shown in the previous project. The rounded corners give this timepiece a more traditional look.

④

2"

1" R

5/16" DP

1 3/8" dia.

1/8" R

2 7/8"

3/4"

1/2"

2 3/4"

1 1/8"

FRONT VIEW

SIDE VIEW

Special instructions

- Use the plans at full size. Choose a nice hardwood and cut pieces to overall size. Locate and drill a 1 3/8-inch-diameter hole, 5/16 deep for the insert.
- Use a 1/8 radius router bit with a follower to make the cut for the base.
- Round the top section.
- Carefully glue the top section to the base as shown—take care not to let glue squeeze out over the base.
- Add four 1/2-inch-diameter felt pad feet (not shown).
- Use a 1 7/16" dia. mini insert (Merritt's Antiques P-1273).

INSERTS: CHERRY TREE TOYS

This project serves three functions: It holds business cards, tells the time and records the temperature. Be sure to make it out of a very special wood. Walnut, cherry or any unusual kind of wood is a good choice. This sample was made of cocobolo wood. You might want to use doll house hinges and catch if you can find them. Try using epoxy to anchor the hinges and latch in place rather than using short brass screws.

Special instructions

- Use the plans at full size.
- Choose special wood.
- Cut the wood to an overall size of $2^3/4$" x $4^1/2$".
- In part No. 1, drill two 1 3/8-inch-diameter by 3/8-inch- deep holes.
- In part No. 2, cut out the center section.
- Glue part No. 2 to part No. 3 and sand the edges.
- Attach two hinges, part No. 4.
- Sand all over.
- Attach clasp, part No. 5.
- Add lid stop, No. 9.
- Re-sand and stain to suit.
- Add the clock and a thermometer.
- Add felt pads to the bottom.

ASSEMBLY VIEW

Hinge 3/4" x 15/32" ⑨

⑥ ⑦

TOP VIEW

⑤

9

1/2" TK

4 1/2"

Small clasp 1" x 3/4"

① ②

FRONT VIEW ③

1 3/8"

2 3/4"

④

9

SIDE VIEW ⑧

①

1/2"

②

3/4"

③

1/8"

4 1/2"

2 3/4"

No.	Name	Size	Req'd
1	Lid	1/2" x 2 3/4" – 4 1/2"	1
2	Body	3/4" x 2 3/4" – 4 1/2"	1
3	Bottom	1/8" x 2 3/4" – 4 1/2"	1
4	Hinge-butt	3/4" x 15/32"	1 pr.
5	Clasp, small	1" x 3/4"	1
6	Clock insert	1 7/16" dia.	1
7	Therm. insert	1 7/16" dia.	1
8	Felt pad	1 1/2" dia.	4
9	Lid stop	1/2" x 3/8" – 3/4"	1

Fit-up clock – Cherry Tree Toys: 57-106AA
Fit-up thermometer – Cherry Tree Toys: 13-113 (1 7/16" Dia.)

1 1/4" 2" 1 1/4"

①

1 3/8" dia.
3/8" DP
1 3/8" dia.
3/8" DP

2 3/4"

INSIDE VIEW

4 1/2"

1/4" 1/4"

②

3/16"

CUT OUT

3/16"

TOP VIEW

4 1/2"

Full Size

BEZEL/DIAL, MOVEMENT, HANDS: STEEBAR CORP.

This octagon-shaped clock makes a simple, but beautifully designed wall clock. It is a one-piece project that will add elegance to any room. This sample was made of red oak. Try to use 7/8-inch-thick wood, if you can find it.

Brass hanger

8" dia. dial & bezel

10¹/₂" square

Quartz movement 2¹/₈" square

FRONT VIEW

SIDE VIEW

ASSEMBLY VIEW

Special instructions

- Use a photocopier to enlarge the plans to 165%.
- Find a piece of hardwood with an interesting grain pattern.
- Cut the wood to an overall size of 10 ¹/₂" x 10 ¹/₂".
- From the back, use a 3-inch-diameter Forstner bit to drill a ³/₈-inch-deep hole at the exact center.
- Cut off the 4 diagonal corners. Sand all over.
- Using a ¹/₄-inch-radius router bit with a follower, cut the concave radius all around the outside edge, as shown.
- Sand all over. Stain to suit.
- Attach the dial face and bezel using small brass tacks.
- Add the movement, hands and hanger. (Steebar Corp.: Bezel/dial 200 mm (8" dia.), Movement A-5, Hands no. 1).

SIDE VIEW

Enlarge 130%

3/4" to 1" tk.

5/8"

10 1/2" sq.

1/4" R

3/8" dia. hole

3" Dia. hole (from rear – use a forstner bit) – 5/8" DP

FRONT VIEW

If you need a wall clock for a modern setting, this clock is just right. It is a small, one-piece clock.

FRONT VIEW

3" dia. x $^3/_8$" deep
(from back)

Movement

SIDE VIEW

Enlarge 165%

Special instructions

- Use a photocopier to enlarge the plans to 165%.
- Choose an interesting piece of hardwood.
- Locate the exact center and drill a $^5/_{16}$-inch-diameter hole from the front to the back.
- From the center of the $^5/_{16}$-inch-diameter hole and from the back of the piece, drill a 3-inch-diameter, $^3/_8$-inch-deep hole with a Forstner bit.

- Make a copy of the face pattern, enlarging it to 165%. Glue to wood.
- Make all the interior cuts.
- Sand.
- Apply a clear coat top finish.
- Add the movement with the hanger attached.
- Add the hands and the battery.
- Material: $^3/_4$" x 10$^1/_4$" – 10$^1/_4$" (Movement: Klockit No. 10004, Hands no. 27).

MOVEMENT AND HANDS: KLOCKIT CO.

This is a wall clock for the deer hunter. It will surely be a hit for your den or play-room. The sample clock was made of avodire on walnut.

Special instructions

- Use a photocopier to enlarge the plans 165%.
- Choose two kinds of wood: a light wood and a contrasting, darker wood. (Try using a light and dark stain if contrasting woods are not available.)
- Attach pattern to the $1/4$-inch-thick wood and cut it out.
- Cut a $3/4$-inch-thick backboard to $9^1/2$-inch-diameter.

- From the back, drill a $3^1/2$-inch-diameter, $1/2$-inch-deep hole. With the $3^1/2$-inch-diameter hole as the center point, start at the back and drill a $5/16$-inch-diameter hole through to the front.
- Sand all over. Stain to suit.
- Glue the front cut out to the backboard.
- Add the movement, hanger and hands (Movement: Klockit No. 10043, Hands no. 27).

3/8" dia. dowel – 5/16" long
12 required (paint black)

⑤

Cut pattern
in 1/4" thick
front piece
only

②

③

9 1/2" dia.

①

3" dia.
1/2" dp.

MOVEMENT
W/ HANGER

④

Dark
stain
back
piece

②

③

FRONT VIEW

Sand edge after assembly

Enlarge 165%

3/4"

1/4"

SIDE VIEW

3" dia. 1/2" deep (from back)

①

②

④

⑤

③

EXPLODED VIEW

3/8" dia. hole (30° apart) 12 places

MOVEMENT, PEN, PENCIL, INSERT: STEEBAR

This project adds class to any desk. It incorporates a clock, pen and pencil all wrapped up into one modern desk clock. The sample clock was made of walnut.

Special instructions

- Choose an interesting hardwood. Cut it to size according to the cutting list.
- Follow the detail drawings to make all the pieces.
- In Part No. 2, drill a 2 3/8-inch-diameter, 1/2-inch-deep hole using a Forstner.
- Sand all over. Stain to suit.
- Screw the post No. 2 to the base No. 1.
- Add the pen/pencil set.
- Add the insert and the felt pad feet.

FRONT VIEW

7³/₄"

2¹/₄"

SIDE VIEW

3"

No.	Name	Size	Req'd
1	Base	⁵/₈" x 3" – 7³/₄"	1
2	Post	1¹/₂" x 3¹/₂" – 5¹/₈"	1
3	Pen/pencil set	To suit	1
4	Fl. hd. screw	#5 - 1¹/₄"lg.	2
5	Fl. hd. machine screw	To suit	2
6	Pad - felt	¹/₂" dia.	4

Steebar: JR pen, JR pencil, E-72 MM movement, Arabic

EXPLODED VIEW

1³/4" radius

2³/8" dia. ¹/2" deep

9/16"

5¹/8"

3³/8"

¹/8" dia. hole
¹/2" deep

¹7/32"   2⁷/16"   ¹7/32"

3¹/2"

5/8"

1¹/2"

¹/8" dia. hole – countersink from bottom 4 places

5/8"

1¹/2"

3"

1⁵/32"   1¹/2"   2⁷/16"   1¹/2"   1⁵/32"

7³/4"

¹/4" R.

5/8"

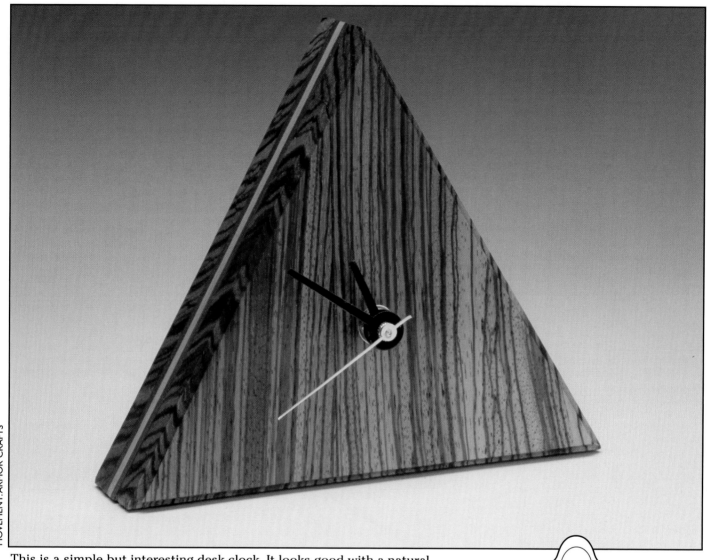

MOVEMENT: ARMOR CRAFTS

This is a simple but interesting desk clock. It looks good with a natural finish or painted. The model clock was made of zebra wood on purpleheart with pau amarello in the center.

Special instructions

- Cut the triangle from a 1³/₄-inch-thick piece of wood. (If you can't find wood that inch thick, glue up two ³/₄-inch-thick pieces sandwiched between one ¹/₄-inch-thick piece.
- Cut the triangle to size and sand all over.
- Make a ¹/₈-inch radius contour around the front (optional) using a router bit with a follower.
- From the back, drill a 3³/₈-inch-diameter 1-inch-deep hole.
- Sand all over. Stain or paint to suit.
- Add felt pads.
- Add a movement with batteries.
- Add the hands.

No.	Name	Size	Req'd
1	Body	1³/₄" x 5³/₄" – 6⁵/₈"	1
2	Quartz movement	Long stem	1
3	Hands (1¹/₂" size)	Modern style	1 pr.
4	Foot	¹/₂" size	4

Movement: Armor Crafts No. 22203 with No. 816 hands

FRONT VIEW

3¹⁵/₁₆"

6⁵/₈"

3¹⁵/₁₆"

3/8" dia. hole – thru from front

1³/₄" time ring

3³/₈" dia. hole – 1" deep (from back)

1⁵/₁₆"

5³/₄"

SIDE VIEW

1³/₄"

1/8" radius

Here is an unusual desk or shelf clock. It should be made of a nice hardwood. This model clock was made of goncolo alves wood.

TOP VIEW

6¹/₄"

FRONT VIEW

5"

¼" dia. hole – thru
2 places in line

⅛" R all around

5⅝"

1¹¹/₁₆" R

1

5/8" dia. hole

FRONT VIEW

1¼"

¼" dia. hole
5/8" deep
2 places

4³/₈"

Full size

No.	Name	Size	Req'd
1	Support	³/₄" x 4¹/₄" – 6¹/₈"	1
2	Doughnut	1 x 3¹/₂" – 3¹/₂"	1
3	Base	³/₄" x 2" – 5"	1
4	Insert	2¹³/₁₆" dia.	1
5	Peg	¹/₄" dia. – 1" lg.	2
6	Foot - felt	¹/₂" dia.	4
7	Pin	¹/₄" dia. – 1¹/₄" lg.	2
Movement: Klockit Co. No. 15223			

1/4" dia. hole – 2 places

2"

TOP VIEW

5"

3

1/8" radius

FRONT VIEW

Full size

3 1/4" dia.

1"

1/8" radius

1/4" dia. hole(2)
1/2" deep

2

2 3/8" dia.

7/8" deep

Special instructions

• Use the plans at full size.
• Choose a nice hardwood.
• In part No. 2, use a Forstner bit to drill a 2³/8-inch-diameter, ⁷/8-inch-deep hole.
• Drill all holes and sand all pieces.
• Assemble and stain to suit.
• Add top clear coat.
• Install insert.
• Add four felt feet.

This clock design is taken from an original antique clock. It is an interesting design and will add a little formality to any room. The model clock was made of purpleheart wood.

2³/₈" dia. hole ⁷/₈" deep or to suit

3³/₄"

Dial face 3⁵/₁₆" dia.

2"

④

①

6⁷/₈"

1⁵/₈" radius

①

6¹/₈"

4³/₁₆"

1⁵/₈"

1¹¹/₁₆"

1/8" R

3⁵/₈"

¹/₄"

②

3/8"

③

③

³/₄" dia. foot

2¹/₄"

2¹/₄"

FRONT VIEW

SIDE VIEW

Enlarge 130%

No.	Name	Size	Req'd
1	Body	¹/₂" x 4" – 6¹/₄"	4
2	Base	³/₈" x 2¹/₄" – 4"	1
3	Foot (³/₄" dia.)		4
4	Insert		1

Steebar Corp.: 3¹/₄" dia. movement No. BFU-R-26
Merritt's Antiques: brass feet No. P-951-A

Special instructions

- Glue four ¹/₂-inch-thick pieces of wood together for the 2-inch-thick body. (4" x 6¹/₄")
- Use a photocopier to enlarge the pattern 130%.
- Drill a 2 ³/₈-diameter hole, ⁷/₈-inches-deep for the insert.
- Make the base as shown and attach the body assembly.
- Sand all over and stain to suit.
- Apply a clear top coat.
- Add four ³/₄-inch-diameter feet.
- Add the insert with batteries.

This clock is truly modern and will really make the setting for modern décor. It is unusual. Pau almarello and morado wood was used in making this clock.

FRONT VIEW

③ 3/16" radius

CUT OUT

SIDE VIEW

4 1/2" dia.

9 3/4"

7 1/2"

Notch for body ①
3/4" x 3 3/4"

EXPLODED VIEW

No.	Name	Size	Req'd
1	Body	3/4" x 4 7/8" – 9"	1
2	Face	1/2" x 4 1/2" – 4 1/2"	1
3	Frame	1/4" x 4 1/2" – 4 1/2"	1
4	Base	3/4" x 2 1/2" – 5"	1
5	Foot	3/4" dia. balls	4
6	Brad	1 1/4" long	4
7	Back	1/8" x 4" – 4"	1
8	Movement quartz		1
9	Hands	1 3/4" lg.	1 pr.
10	Screw - rd. hd.	#4 – 5/8" lg.	3

Klockit Co. No. 10004 with No. 7 hands

CUT OUT

$4^{1}/2$" dia.

3" dia.

$2^{15}/16$" R.

$1/4$" radius

CUT OUT

4" R.

1

$4^{11}/16$" R.

$5/16$"

$5/16$"

4

9"

$6^{3}/4$"

$3/4$"

$3^{3}/4$"

$3/4$"

$4^{7}/8$"

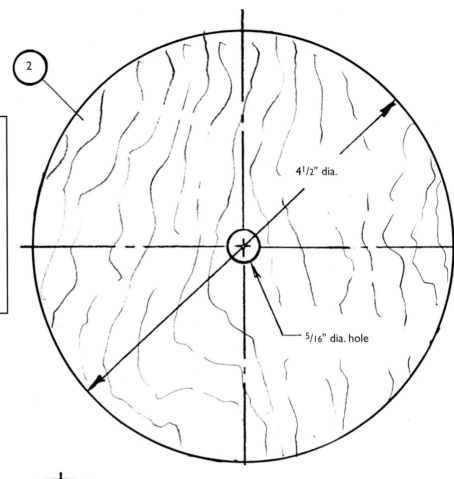

Special instructions

- Transfer the body shape (No. 1) to the wood and cut it out as shown. Sand all over.
- Cut to shape all of the remaining pieces. Sand all the pieces, keeping all edges sharp.
- Assemble and stain to suit.
- Apply a clear top coat.
- Install movement and hands.

②

4¹/2" dia.

⁵/16" dia. hole

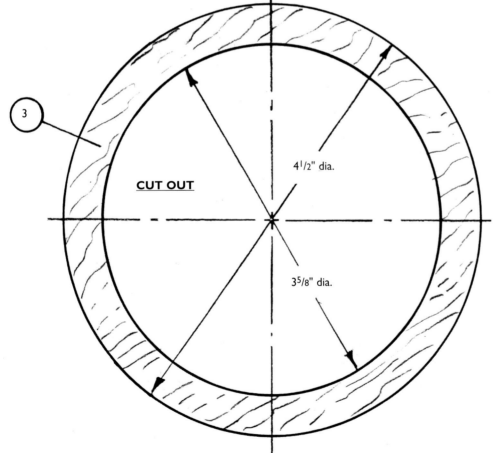

③

4¹/2" dia.

CUT OUT

3⁵/8" dia.

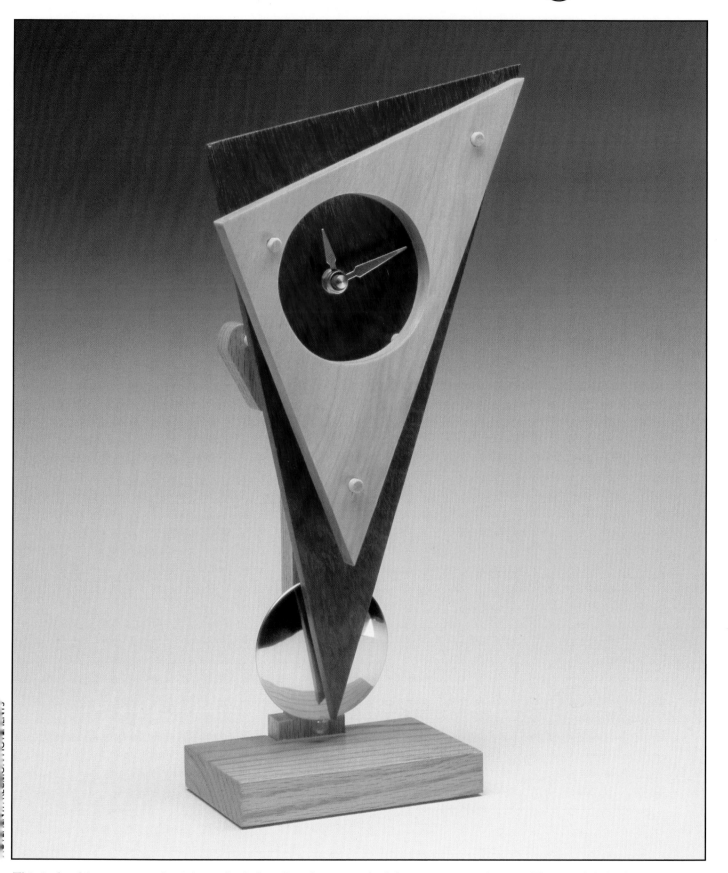

This indeed is an unusual modern clock. It will make a wonderful conversational piece. This model clock was made of pau amarello, purpleheart and red oak.

6³/₈"

2³/₄"

① ②

② ①

③

⑧

⑨

⑨

⑥

6" pend.

② ⑥

④

② 13"

③

2³/₄" dia.

④

⑤

⑤

⑦ ⑦

4³/₄"

3¹/₄"

FRONT VIEW

SIDE VIEW

5/16" dia. hole

1/4" dia. hole

3/8" dia.

3/8"

3

1/4" dia. hole –
1/4" deep
(back surface)
2 places

4

2 5/8"

3" dia.

2 5/8"

1

1/4" dia. hole – 3 places

FRONT VIEW

1/4" dia. hole –
5 places

FRONT VIEW

Enlarge 165%

1 3/8"

5/8"

3 1/4"

7

4 3/4"

FRONT VIEW

5

1 3/8"

2 5/8"

FRONT VIEW

8 1/2"

EXPLODED VIEW

No.	Name	Size	Req'd
1	Blackboard	$3/8$" × $6^5/8$" – 11"	1
2	Pin	$1/4$" dia. – $1^1/4$"	3
3	Spacer	$3/8$" dia. – $3/8$"	1
4	Front	$3/8$" × $6^5/8$" – $7^1/4$"	1
5	Support	$5/8$" × $3^3/8$" – $8^1/2$"	1
6	Peg	$1/4$" dia. – $2^5/8$"	2
7	Base	$3/4$" × $3^1/4$" – $4^3/4$"	1

Movement: Precision Movements No. 1003309 with No. 1008732 hands

MOVEMENT:ARMOR CRAFTS

This clock can be painted or stained to suit to create many variations of the same model.

Face assembly = parts ① ② ③ ④
sand edges after assembly

⑥

Gold nos.

⑧

⑥

⑥

⑦

⑥

Color to
suit

10³/4"

⑥

⑤

⑤

⑤

5/8" | 5/8" | 3¹/2" | 5/8" | 5/8"

6"

FRONT VIEW

①
②
③
④

⑧

⑦

⑤

SIDE VIEW

2⁵/8"

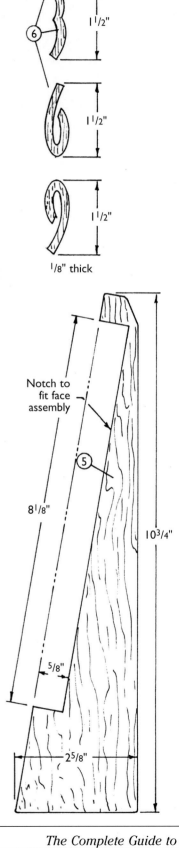

12 — 1¹/2"

⑥ — 1¹/2"

6 — 1¹/2"

9 — 1¹/2"

¹/8" thick

Notch to
fit face
assembly

⑤

8¹/8"

5/8"

10³/4"

2⁵/8"

5/8" thick

No.	Name	Size	Req'd
1	Front	³/16" x 6" – 8¹/8"	1
2	Central	¹/4" x 6" – 8¹/8"	1
3	Back	³/16" x 6" – 8¹/8"	1
4	Mirror	¹/8" x 4" – 6¹/8"	1
5	Leg	5/8" x 2⁵/8" – 10³/4"	2
6	Numbers	¹/8" x 1¹/2" – 4"	4
7	Movement	³/4" shaft length	1
8	Hands	2³/16" to 2¹/2" lg.	1 pr.

Movements: Armor Crafts No. 22203 with 2¹/4" lg. hands

① 3/16" thick

CUT OUT

2"

8 1/8"

4 1/8"

2"

1 3/4" 2 1/2" 1 3/4"

6"

FRONT VIEW

② 1" 1/4" thick

CUT OUT

6 1/8"

1" 4" 1"

6"

FRONT VIEW

③ 3/16" thick

CUT OUT

3" dia.

4 1/16"

8 1/8"

3" 3"

6"

FRONT VIEW

④ 1/8" thick mirror plexiglass

6 1/8"

5/16" dia. hole

3 1/16"

4"

FRONT VIEW

Paint gold

Paint black

EXPLODED VIEW

Special instructions

- Cut all pieces per the cutting list.
- Layout and make all interior cuts per drawings.
- Glue parts No. 1, 2 and 3.
- Sand all edges so the assembly appears to be one piece of wood.
- Cut the Plexiglas mirror to fit.
- Enlarge the three numbers to $1^1/2$ inches high and cut them out.
- Paint numbers gold.
- Paint or stain the face assembly (part No. 1, 2, 3).
- Paint the legs (part No. 5) black.
- Assemble all parts and add a movement with hands.

MOVEMENT: STEEBAR CORP.

Tambour clocks are still in fashion, as they were in 1910. They were one of the most enduring clock designs ever made. Walnut with satinwood accents were used in this clock.

Special instructions

- Either layout the patterns for part No. 1 and 2 or have copies made at 165%.
- Cut out pieces No. 1 and 2 with a band saw and than sand all over.
- Locate and drill a $7/8$ inch deep, $3^1/8$-inch-diameter hole.
- Cut part No. 6 out of a piece of a very unusual piece of $1/8$" x 1" - 5 $7/8$" piece of wood. Stain or paint yellow (optional).
- Assemble the body with the base and stain to suit.
- Locate and glue in place the trim (part No. 6).
- Apply two coats of clear top coat.
- Add the feet and insert.

FRONT VIEW

16³/₄"

7³/₄"

SIDE VIEW

EXPLODED VIEW

No.	Name	Size	Req'd
1	Body	2" x 7" – 16"	1
2	Base	³/₄" x 2³/₈" – 16³/₄"	1
3	Screw-flat head	No. 6 – 1¹/₄"	2
4	Insert clock	6¹/₄" dia.	1
5	Foot	¹/₂" dia.	4

Movement: Steebar Corp. 160MM-FR or 160MM-FA – 6¹/₄" dia.

TOP VIEW

2"

7/8"

FRONT VIEW

3/8"

7"

Enlarge 165%

2¹/8" radius

2¹/8" radius

Yellow paint trim (optional)

3¹/4" radius

7⁵/8"

16"

3¹/8" dia.
× 7/8" deep

6¹/4" dia.
dial face

1

3³/4"

TOP VIEW

Drill and countersink for a no.6 screw

④

1"

23/8"

1/2"

1/2"

④

FRONT VIEW

1"

23/4"

163/4"

② Chamber 1/4" × 45° – 3 sides only

3/32"

Cut as shown

1"

23/8"

TRIM DETAIL

Enlarge 165%

57/8"

33/8" radius

⑥

Full size

This pretty little clock will add warmth to any room. Reminiscent of the Victorian age, it is a great clock for a young girl's room. Our sample was made of white oak with a purpleheart accent. The design is based on an original antique clock.

2¹/₂" x 3¹/₄" oval insert

⑧

①

5³/₄"

⑨

⑤

A

⑥

FRONT VIEW

⑧ ④

⑤

②

⑨

③

A

⑦

SIDE VIEW

ASSEMBLY VIEW

③

②   ②

①

⑨   ⑤

VIEW AT AA

⑧

④

⑧

②

③

⑧

(Trim to fit
at assembly)

②

①

⑤

⑨

2¹/₂" x 3¹/₄" oval
insert (not shown)

⑥

⑦

EXPLODED VIEW

Special instructions

- Use a contrasting wood for part No. 5.
- Make the molding as shown or as close as possible using whatever router bits you have.
- Dry fit all the pieces and adjust if necessary.
- Glue all pieces together.
- Sand all over and apply one or two clear top coats.
- Add the insert.

Movement from: Turncraft No. 5696 – Arabic or 5698 – Roman

4

3⁵/₁₆"

¹/₄"

¹/₈"

1¹³/₁₆"

5

2" 2"

³/₈" R

¹/₈" R ¹/₁₆"

2³/₈" dia.

1¹/₂"

3"

4"

³/₁₆"

Use a contrasting wood for 5

Cut off to 5/16" width after forming

9/16" 5/16"

¹/₁₆" R

8

5/16"

3

3¹/₁₆"

¹/₈"

Make a r.h.–l.h pair of 7

³/₈"

7

1¹³/₁₆"

1¹¹/₁₆"

45°

¹/₁₆"

2³/₁₆"

10" long

2

5"

³/₈"

¹/₈"

¹/₈"

³/₈"

45°

¹/₈"

7/8"

6

3⁵/₁₆"

1

5"

³/₈"

¹/₈"

2⁹/₁₆"

³/₈"

¹/₈"

2³/₈" dia.

3⁵/₁₆"

2³/₈"

2⁵/₈"

45°

³/₁₆" R

4¹/₁₆"

Trim to suit at assembly

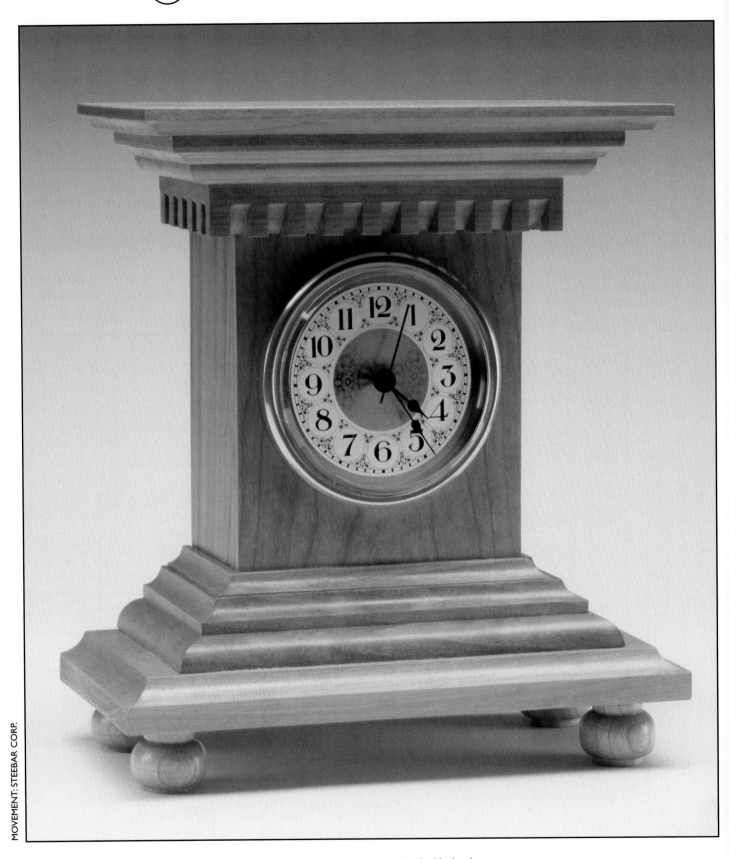

MOVEMENT: STEEBAR CORP.

If you like antique projects, you will really like this pretty, original shelf clock.

FRONT VIEW

8 1/4"

7"

1" dia.

SIDE VIEW

3 7/8"

VIEW AT A-A

1/8"

No.	Name	Size	Req'd
1	Front dentil	3/8" x 1 1/4" – 4 3/4" lg.	1
2	Side dentil	3/8" x 1 1/4" – 2 3/4" lg.	2
3	Face	3/8" x 4" – 6 5/8" lg.	1
4	Side	3/8" x 2 1/4" – 6 5/8" lg.	2
5	Back (pine)	1/8" x 3 5/8" – 6 5/8" lg.	1
6	Trim bottom	3/8" x 1" – 12" lg.	1
7	Trim bottom	5/8" x 5/8" – 16" lg.	1
8	Base	1/2" x 3 7/8" – 7" lg.	1
9	Trim top	3/4" x 3/4" – 18" lg.	1
10	Top	3/8" x 3 7/8" – 7" lg.	1
11	Foot	1" dia. x 1 1/8" lg.	4
12	Insert		1

Movement: Steebar Corp. No. BFU-A-21

Special instructions

- Use a photocopier to enlarge the pattern 165%.
- Study the exploded view so you will know how it all goes together.
- Cut all the pieces to overall size and sand the front and back surfaces.
- Make all parts per the detailed drawings and the exploded view.
- The 4 feet (part No. 11) can be turned or purchased. One-inch-diameter ball feet could be substituted if necessary.
- Dry fit all pieces.
- Sand all pieces.
- If everything fits correctly, assemble the pieces.
- Apply a stain (optional) and three clear top coats.
- Install the insert.

Enlarge 165%

45°   45°

TOP VIEW

4³/₄"

①

FRONT VIEW

3/8"

1¹/₄"

1/4"

END VIEW

45°

¹/₄" wide dentil work

45°

TOP VIEW

2³/₄"

②

FRONT VIEW

3/8"

1¹/₄"

1/4"

END VIEW

45°

⑪

1"   5/8"

1/4"   5/8"

9/16"   3/8"
3/16"
1¹/₈"

FRONT VIEW

¹/₄" radius

END VIEW

1"

3/8"

⑥   Trim to suit

FRONT VIEW

12"

3/16"

³/₁₆" radius
⁵/₁₆" radius

5/8"

END VIEW   5/8"

⑦   Trim to suit

FRONT VIEW

16"

¹/₄" radius

³/₈" radius

3/4"

⑨   Trim to suit

FRONT VIEW

3/4"

END VIEW

18"

Rabbet 1/8" wide x 1/8" deep

Rabbet 3/8" wide x 1/4" deep

1/8"

2 3/8" dia. hole – or to suit

1/4" dia. hole – 4 places

3/4"

3/4"

3/4"

3 7/8"

EXPLODED VIEW

DIAL/BEZEL, MOVEMENT, HANDS, FEET, ORNAMENTS: KLOCKIT CO.

This clock is an exact copy of an original antique black mantel clock. You still can get copies of the original lion heads, feet and trim. Originals actually had wonderful movements. A good wood choice would be yellow poplar painted with black lacquer.

SIDE VIEW

FRONT VIEW

3⅜"

6⅜"

7¼"

EXPLODED VIEW

3 1/2" dia, hole

No.	Name	Size	Req'd
1	Front	1/2" x 4 3/4"–6 1/4"	1
2	Side	1/2" x 3"–6 1/4"	2
3	Back (pine)	1/4" x 3 3/4"–6 1/4"	1
4	Top/bottom (pine)	1/4" x 2 1/4"–3 3/4"	2
5	Base (cut to size)	3/4" x 1 5/8"–16"	1
6	Top	1/2" x 3"–4 3/4"	1
7	Bottom molding	7/16" x 9/16"–16"	1
8	Top molding	1/2" x 1/2"–16"	1
9	Foot	38243 (H)	1 set
10	Lion Head	38007 (D)	2
11	Ornament	38285 (Y)	1
12	Movement quartz	10004	1
13	Dial/bezel	3 1/4" to 3 1/2" dia.- 27006	1
14	Hands	66983	1 pair

Parts Nos. 9 to 14 from Klockit Co.

Special instructions

- Make moldings as close as possible to the design illustrated.
- Dry fit all the pieces as you go.
- Sand all the pieces, taking care to keep sharp edges.
- Assemble and glue the pieces together.
- Apply 3 or 4 coats of primer, sanding between each coat. Original black mantel clocks had a beautiful glass-like finish.
- Apply two coats of high gloss, black lacquer.
- Add the feet, trim and dial/bezel.
- Add the movement with hands.
- Apply a coat of butcher wax.

MOVEMENT: STEEBAR CORP.

This clock makes a great kitchen clock. It can be stained or painted to match the room. The drawer gives you a little added storage space. A nice wood choice would be butternut because of its unusual character.

Rabbet ¹/₄" wide - ¹/₄" deep

³/₄"

⁵

⁶

2¹/₄"

³

¹/₈" bead (optional)

VIEW AT A-A

4¹/₂"

2³/₄"

⁷

⁴

¹/₂"

2¹/₂"

8¹/₂"

2¹/₂"

1³/₄"

¹/₂"

³/₄"

FRONT VIEW

4¹/₂"

6"

SIDE VIEW

2¹/₄"

3"

EXPLODED VIEW

2³/8" dia. hole or dia. to suit

No.	Name	Size	Req'd
1	Side	³/4" x 2¹/4"–7¹/4"	2
2	Sub-base	¹/2" x 2¹/4"–3¹/4"	1
3	Front	³/4" x 3¹/4"–5"	1
4	Brad	³/4" lg.	as req'd
5	Back	¹/4" x 3³/4"–7"	1
6	Base	³/4" x 3"–6"	1
7	Top	¹/2" x 2³/4"–5¹/2"	1
8	Drawer - front	³/8" x 1³/4"–3¹/4"	1
9	Drawer - side	¹/4" x 1³/4"–2"	2
10	Drawer - back	¹/4" x 1³/4"–3"	1
11	Drawer - bottom	¹/4" x 1⁵/8"–2³/4"	1
12	Drawer- pull	¹/2" dia.	1
13	Movement - quartz	3¹/4" dia.	1
14	Foot - felt	¹/2" dia.	4

Movement: Steebar Corp. No. BFU-A-27 with black bezel (3¹/4" dia.)

Special instructions

- Cut and fit all pieces per the exploded view and assembly views.
- Dry fit all pieces.
- If the fit is correct, glue the pieces together.
- Fit the drawer to the opening.
- Sand all over.
- Stain or paint to suit.
- Add the feet and insert.

MOVEMENT: THE AMERICAN CLOCK CO.; DIAL FACE: SHIPLEY CO.

Due to their popularity, we have included two mission mantel clocks. These clocks were popular in the last part of the 1800s. Today oak clocks are back in popularity. Your clock should be made of red oak as the one illustrated in the photograph, if at all possible.

FRONT VIEW

5"

12"

7 1/4"

SIDE VIEW

3 3/8"

½"

4°

4

Make
a r.h.-
l.h.
pair

11"

EDGE VIEW

⅛"

¼"

2⅞"

3/8"

END VIEW

4¾"

¼" dia. hole
6 places

2⅝"

10⅞"

1¼"

a

CUT OUT

a

5

¼"

3½"

¼"

4°

⅛"

⅛"

¼" thick

FRONT VIEW

6¼"

6⅜"

1"

6

¼" thick

1⅝"

1⅞"

¼"

FRONT VIEW

1¼"

2⅝"

No.	Name	Size	Req'd
1	Front	$1/2" \times 6^{1}/2" - 10^{7}/8"$	1
2	Glass - top	$4^{7}/16"$ dia.	1
3	Glass - bottom	$2^{7}/16"$ dia.	1
4	Side (rh/lh)	$1/2" \times 2^{7}/8" - 11"$	2
5	Back	$1/4" \times 6^{1}/4" - 10^{7}/8"$	1
6	Vertical support	$1/4" \times 1^{7}/8" - 6^{3}/8"$	2
7	Dial support	$1/8" \times 4^{11}/16" - 5"$	1
8	Dial face (paper)	$3^{1}/2"$ dia.	1
9	Bottom	$5/8" \times 3^{3}/8" - 7^{1}/4"$	1
10	Top	$1/2" \times 3^{3}/8" - 5^{7}/8"$	1
11	Finish nails	#4d	4
12	Hands	$1^{5}/8"$ lg (#24)	1 pr.
13	Quartz movement	5" pend. length	1
14	Foot - felt	$1/2"$ dia.	4
15	Screw - rd. hd.	No. 6 – $5/8"$ lg.	6

Movement: The American Clock Company No. C2306 H48
with No. 2450 hands (cut to fit)
Dial face: Shipley Co. A3500

5"

A

CUT OUT

4" dia.

2⁵/₈"

1/4"R

5"

10⁷/₈"

1/4"

CUT OUT

2" dia.

1/4"R

3¹/₄"

1/4"

FRONT VIEW

A

1/2"

1/2"

VIEW AT A-A

1/2"

1/8"

1/2"

BOTTOM VIEW

6¹/₂"

⑫ hands
⑬ movement

paper dial

EXPLODED VIEW

Special instructions

- Make all pieces per the detail drawings and sand all over.
- Dry fit all the pieces.
- Add glass. Hold it in place with black putty.
- Glue the pieces together. Do not glue back (No. 5) with vertical support (No. 6) attached. Screw these pieces in place.
- Stain to suit and apply a clear top coat.
- Add the four ¹/₂-inch-diameter feet.
- Add the movement and hands.

MOVEMENT: PRECISION MOVEMENT

This clock is a copy of an early Mission clock from 1910 or so. It is simply a box with legs. Consider making this model of red oak like the clock pictured in the photograph.

Rabbet 3/16" wide x 3/32" deep

3/16"

3/16"

3/16"

2⁹/₁₆"

15

2

8

2

8

7/8"

5/8"

4

3

13

3¼" dia.

14

1

5³/₄"
Box Size

12

4"

3

7

9¹/₂"

7

2

1¹/₈"

2

2

1¹/₂"

6

9

6

5/8"

11

8

10

5

5

3/4"

11

5

5/8"   4"   5/8"

7/16"   3/4" 5/8" 3/4" 5/8"

5¹/₄"

3³/₁₆"

FRONT VIEW

SIDE VIEW

Rabbet ³/₁₆" wide x ³/₃₂" deep

EXPLODED VIEW

No.	Name	Size	Req'd
1	Case side	³/₁₆" x 2⁹/₁₆" − 5³/₄" lg.	2
2	Case top/bottom	³/₁₆" x 2⁹/₁₆" − 4⁷/₈" lg.	2
3	Face	³/₁₆" x 4¹/₂" − 5³/₈" lg.	1
4	Back	³/₁₆" x 4⁷/₈" − 5³/₄" lg.	1
5	Post - front	⁷/₁₆" x ⁵/₈" − 9¹/₂" lg.	2
6	Top/bottom rail	³/₁₆" x ⁵/₈" − 4" lg.	2
7	Center rail	³/₁₆" x 1¹/₈" − 4" lg.	1
8	Post - side	³/₁₆" x ⁵/₈" − 9¹/₂" lg.	4
9	Side brace	³/₁₆" x ⁵/₈" − 2⁹/₁₆" lg.	2
10	Back brace	³/₁₆" x ⁵/₈" − 4⁷/₈" lg.	1
11	Corner brace	³/₈" x ³/₈" − ⁵/₈" lg.	4
12	Brass tack	¹/₄" lg.	60
13	Numbers (gold)	³/₈" high	1 set
14	Movement	To suit	1
15	Hands	1¹/₂" lg.	1 set
16	Brad	¹/₂" lg.	as req'd

Movement: Precision Movement
No. 1003210 - Hands
No. 1008518 - ³/₈" numbers
No. 102238

Special instructions

- Study the exploded view.
- Note the rabbet on the two sides (part No. 1).
- Make a simple box with parts No. 1, 2, 3 and 4.
- Make up a sub-assembly of parts No. 5, 6 and 7.
- Attach this sub-assembly with the box and add the legs (No. 8). Glue and nail with small brads. Cut to fit and add parts No. 9, 10 and 11.
- Using full-size tack layout, add 60 tacks (part No. 12).
- Add the movement and hands.

MOVEMENT: KLOCKIT CO.

Years ago Skeleton clocks were very popular. Most were made by hand. They were made from solid $1/8$-inch-thick brass plates that were actually the side plates for the mechanical brass movement. This is a take off of an early Skeleton clock, but incorporates an assembled brass movement #13010, exclusive from the Klockit Company. This clock will be a great "conversation piece." A high quality $1/4$-inch-thick baltic birch plywood was used to give a "modern" look.

FRONT VIEW

SIDE VIEW

Special instructions

- Use a photocopier to enlarge the pattern to 200%.
- Cut all the pieces to overall size and sand all surfaces.
- Attach the pattern to the wood, drill all 1/4-inch-diameter holes and cut them out.
- Make the base (part No. 7). Notch at "C" for tab the tab (parts No. 1 and 2).
- Cut parts 4, 5A and 5B.
- Put all the pieces together with pins. Do not use glue at this point.
- Glue tabs "C" into the base.
- Stain to suit and add a clear top coat
- Add the movement assembly.

ASSEMBLY

1/16" dia. hole 4 places

3

TOP VIEW

UP

6

D

B

B

B

2

Enlarge 200%

B

B

1/4" dia. hole
7 places

A   A

B

B

B   B

C   C

FRONT VIEW

No.	Name	Size	Req'd
1	Back	1/4" x 13 – 14 1/2"	1
2	Front	1/4" x 13 – 14 1/2"	1
3	Support	1/4" x 3 – 4 1/4"	1
4	Dowel	1/4" dia. – 4" lg.	7
5a	Spacer	1/4" I.D. – 1 7/8"	1
5b	Spacer	1/4" I.D. – 13/16"	12
6	Center Section	1/4" x 5" – 9 1/4"	2
7	Base	3/4" x 3 5/8" – 14 1/4"	1
8	Pin	1/16" dia. – 5/8"	18
9	Foot	1/2" dia.	4
10	Movement	13010	1
Movement from: Klockit Co. 13010			

Enlarge 200%

1/4" dia. hole
7 places

FRONT VIEW

Chamfer ends

3"

B

4

B

1/16" dia.
2 places

5a

1 7/8"

Brass

5b

13/16"

Brass

TOP VIEW

7

C

C

C

C

Mortise 7/16" deep – 4 places

3/16" radius

FRONT VIEW

C

C

1/16" dia. hole 1/2" deep
4 places

1/2" dia.
foot.

This See-Thru Wall Clock is easy to make and can be stained or painted. For a very interesting clock try an exotic wood such as lacewood with a walnut back, like the clock made for this book.

FRONT VIEW

VIEW AT A-A

20"

11¹/₂"
Pend. lg.

9¹/₂"

1¹/₂"

CUT OUT

19"

2¹/₂"

6¹/₂"

9¹/₈"

7/₈"

2¹/₂"

1/₂"

3¹/₂"

7¹/₂"

8¹/₂"

2¹/₂"

1/₂"

1/₂" radius

1" radius

③

1/₄" radius

3/₄"

20"

4³/₄"

8³/₈"

1³/₄"

1¹/₄"

7" dia.

CUT OUT

1" radius

CUT OUT

7"

1¹/₂" radius

9¹/₂"

1¹/₄"

1¹/₄"

①

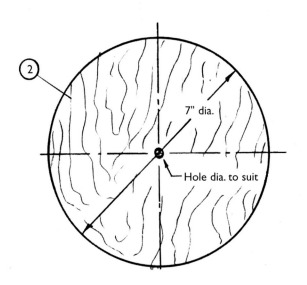

7" dia.

Hole dia. to suit

Special instructions

- Use the pattern at full size.
- Cut all the pieces to overall size.
- Layout the front (part No. 1) and back (part No. 3).
- Cut out the spacer (part No. 2) and drill the hole in center
- Using a 1/4"-inch-radius router bit with a follower, round all edges on part No. 1, as shown.
- Sand all over and stain to suit.
- Glue the dial face to the back (part No. 3).
- Glue everything together and stain or paint.
- Add the movement with the hands.

EXPLODED VIEW

No.	Name	Size	Req'd
1	Front	3/4" x 9 1/2" – 20"	1
2	Spacer	1/2" x 7" – 7"	1
3	Back	3/4" x 8 1/2" – 19"	1
4	Paper dial face	6" minute ring – 7" dia.	1
5	Movement w/ pendulum	11 1/2" pendulum length	1
6	Hands	3" length	1 pr.

Dial face: Shipley Co. – No. A6000
Movement: Cherry Tree Toys – No. 57-109P
Hands: Cherry Tree Toys – No. 66932

This simple clock will add a genuine New England flare to any room. It is a simple clock to make. If you don't have equipment to make the frame (part No. 1), most building supply companies have a molding that matches the profile of part No. 1. This project can be stained or painted. The dial face will brighten up the whole room. Any wood can be used; mahogany is used here.

FRONT VIEW

13¹/₂"

13¹/₂"

VIEW AT A-A

¹/₄"
1³/₄"
3/16"
1¹/₄"
1¹/₂"
10"
1¹/₂"
1³/₄"
¹/₄"

EXPLODED VIEW

Special instructions

- Use the pattern at full size.
- Cut the pieces to size according to the cutting list. Sand all over.
- Use the section view to make the frame piece from $3/4$" x $1^3/4$" x 72" wood. Make 45-degree cuts, 13 inches long. Glue together.
- Make 45-degree cuts at all four corners for the spline and glue the spline in place.
- Add the trim around the perimeter.
- Sand all over and stain or paint to suit.
- Apply a clear top coat.
- Add the dial. Hold in place with the insert (part No. 5).
- Add the movement with hanger, then add the hands.

No.	Name	Size	Req'd
1	Frame	$3/4$" x $1^3/4$" – 13"	4
2	Trim	$1/4$" x $1^1/4$" – $13^1/2$"	4
3	Spline	$1/8$" x $3/4$" – $1^1/4$"	4
4	Dial face	$7^1/2$" time ring	1
5	Insert	$1/4$" x $1/2$" – 11"	4
6	Movement	Quartz	1
7	Moon hands	$3^1/8$" size	1 pr.

Dial – Klockit Co. No. 26041; Movement – Klockit Co. No. 10043; Hands – Klockit Co. No. 22 or equal

FRAME DETAIL(make-up 72")

BEZEL, MOVEMENT, HANDS: STEEBAR CORP.

From the turn of the century, Schoolhouse clocks were hung in every class room throughout the country. I can remember sitting in class listening the tick-tock sound, all day. The janitor would come in with a step ladder and wind it once, every week. Today, you can have a taste of these wonderful old clocks. The original Schoolhouse clocks were made of red oak, as is our sample.

FRONT VIEW

VIEW AT A-A

No.	Name	Size	Req'd
1	Front	3/4" x 10" – 14⁵/8"	1
2	Hands	3¹/8" size	1 pr.
3	Side	¹/2" x 1" – 7" lg.	2
4	Top/bottom	¹/2" x 1" – 6" lg.	2
5	Brad	1" lg.	12
6	Hanger - brass	To suit	1
7	Screw - rd. hd.	As required	2
8	Bezel w. dial face	6³/4" dia.	1
9	Movement w/ pendulum		1

Clock parts from Steebar Corp.: Bezel – 174 mm (6³/4" dia. - Arabic); Movement – APM-15; Hands – 46

10"

2^{15/16"} 4^{1/8"} 2^{15/16"}

2^{15/16"}

4^{1/8"}

5/16" dia. hole

6^{3/4"} dial face

2^{1/4"}

14^{5/8"}

1/4" radius
all edges
(front surface)

3^{1/2"}

5^{5/16"}

CUT OUT

3^{5/8"}

Enlarge 165%

1^{5/8"}

1^{5/8"} 2^{1/4"} 1^{5/8"}

5^{1/2"}

Notch for hanger ⑥

⑤

④

⑥

⑦

③

①

⑤

⑨

③

④

②

⑤

Notch for pendulum

EXPLODED VIEW

⑧
6³/4" dia. bezel with
dial face (not shown)

Special instructions

- Cut all the pieces to overall size
  according to the cutting list.
- Enlarge the pattern to 165%.
- Layout the front (part No. 1).
- Cut out the front and round all edges
  using a $^1/4$-inch router bit with a fol-
  lower.
- Drill a $^5/16$-inch-diameter hole.
- Sand all over and stain to suit.
- Make a box from parts No. 3, 4 and 5.
  Make a notch for the brass hanger
  (part No. 6) and pendulum.
- Glue box to the back of the front.
- Apply a clear top coat.
- Add the dial/bezel.
- Add the movement with batteries.
- Add the hands.

MOVEMENT, DIAL, FACE: KLOCKIT CO.

This clock is very functional. It will tell you the time and provide shelf space for your favorite collection. It looks great stained or painted. If you paint it, you might want to distress it to give it a worn "country" look. Try to use a hardwood if you can. This one is made from maple.

3/8" radius

16"

34"

18"

9" dia.

12 11 10 9 8 7 6 5 4 3 2 1

FRONT VIEW

SIDE VIEW

12 1/4"

4 1/2"

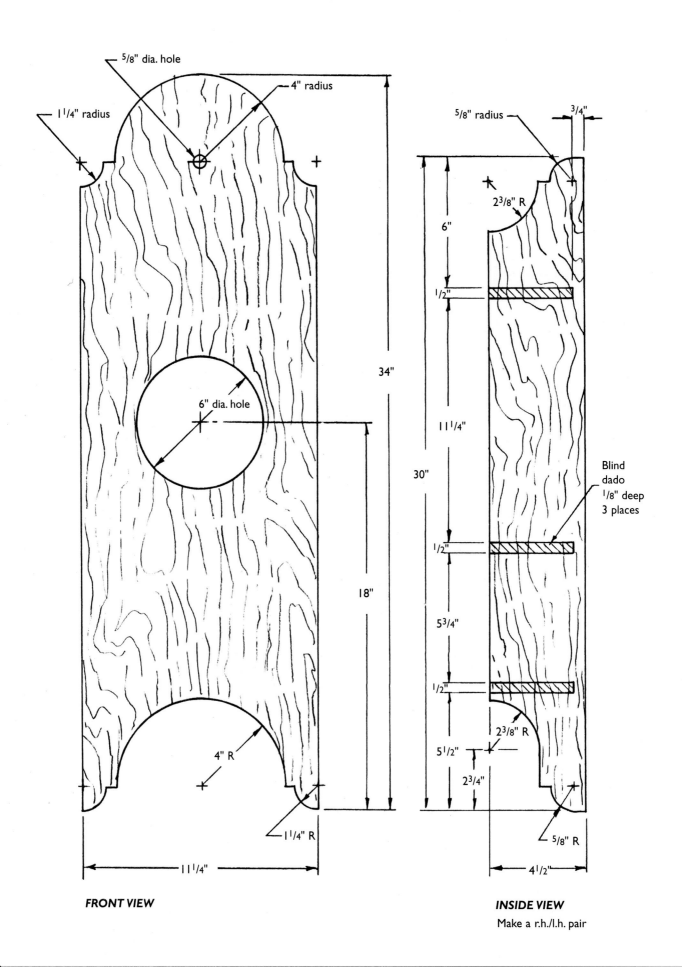

⁵/₈" dia. hole

1¹/₄" radius

4" radius

⁵/₈" radius

³/₄"

2³/₈" R

6"

¹/₂"

34"

Blind
dado
¹/₈" deep
3 places

11¹/₄"

30"

6" dia. hole

¹/₂"

5³/₄"

18"

¹/₂"

2³/₈" R

4" R

5¹/₂"

2³/₄"

1¹/₄" R

⁵/₈" R

11¹/₄"

4¹/₂"

FRONT VIEW

INSIDE VIEW
Make a r.h./l.h. pair

9" dia.

Blind dado
¹/2" wide x
¹/8" deep
3 places

¹/2" wide x
¹/8" deep
¹/8" in from
edge

Dado

EXPLODED VIEW

Special instructions

- Layout the back (part No. 1) and sides (part No. 2).
- Cut out all the pieces and make a right-hand and left-hand pair of sides.
- Carefully make blind dados in the sides (part No. 2).
- Cut dados in the shelves (part No. 3) as shown in the exploded view.
- Dry fit all the pieces and adjust any, if necessary.
- Sand all the pieces, keeping all edges sharp.
- Stain or paint and apply a clear top coat.
- Add glass, face, movement and hands before assembly.
- Glue all the parts together except the backer (part No. 7). Screw it in place.

Notch for glass

End of No. ⑥

No.	Name	Size	Req'd
1	Back	¹/2" x 11¹/4" – 34"	1
2	Side	¹/2" x 4¹/2" – 30"	2
3	Shelf	¹/2" x 4" – 11¹/2"	3
4	Face	¹/2" x 11¹/4" – 11¹/2"	1
5	Glass	10³/4" x – 11¹/8"	1
6	Spacer	¹/2" x 7/8" – 11¹/4"	2
7	Backer	¹/8" x 11³/16" – 11³/16"	1
8	Paper dial	10" size - 8¹/2" time ring	1
9	Screw - rd. hd.	No. 6 – 1¹/4"	4
10	Movement	To suit	1
11	Hands	Klockit No. 66971	1 pr.

Clock parts from: Klockit Co.
Movement – No. 10001
Hands – No. 66971
Paper Dial – No. 26088

MOVEMENT, HANDS, DIAL FACE: PRECISION MOVEMENT

If you have a wide, empty wall, this clock with a shelf is just perfect for you. It will provide you with over 90 inches of shelf space (if you include the top surface). It can be stained or painted and will look great either way. When you get done with this project, you will be an expert on making dados. American chestnut was used for the sample clock.

Special instructions

Special instructions:
• Make all dados, taking care to make exact 90-degree cuts.
• Round the ends of parts No 1, 6 and 7.
• Dry fit all pieces and trim if necessary.
• Glue all pieces together.
• Sand all over.
• Stain or paint and apply a clear top coat.
• Add the bezel, dial face movement and hands.

All dados
1/2" wide × 1/8" deep

73/4" to 8" dia.
dial and bezel

Dia. to suit

1/4" dia. hole - 2 places

3" radius

VIEW AT A-A

FRONT VIEW

10 hands not shown

ASSEMBLY VIEW

Dado ¹/₂" wide x ¹/₈" deep

¹/₄" dia. hole 2 places

Dado ¹/₂" wide x ¹/₈" deep

Rabbet ¹/₂" wide x ¹/₈" deep

No.	Name	Size	Req'd
1	Top/bottom	¹/₂" x 5¹/₂" – 40"	2
2	Vertical board	¹/₂" x 5¹/₂" – 11¹/₄"	2
3	Face	¹/₂" x 11¹/₄" – 11¹/₄"	1
4	Vertical board	¹/₂" x 5¹/₂" – 11¹/₄"	2
5	Backboard	¹/₂" x 4⁵/₈" – 11¹/₄"	2
6	Shelf end	¹/₂" x 5¹/₈" – 4⁵/₈"	2
7	Shelf center	¹/₂" x 5¹/₂" – 9¹/₄"	2
8	Dial - bezel	8" dia	1
9	Quartz movement	To suit (⁵/₈" lg. shaft)	1
10	Hand	To suit	1

Clock parts from Precision Movement:
Movement – No. 1003158
Hands – No. 1008475
Dial Face – No. 1012399 - 8" dia.

For a truly unusual, modern touch, this clock is just perfect. As with many clocks in this book, it will look nice stained or painted. Afrormosia wood was used in making the sample.

Special instructions

- Cut all pieces to overall size and keep everything square.
- Sand all surfaces, keeping sharp corners.
- Make rabbet cuts in the front (part No. 1) and sides (part No. 2).
- Make the cut outs in the sides (part No. 2) and back (part No. 3). Be sure to make a right-hand and left-hand pair of sides.
- Sand again, all over.
- Dry fit all pieces.
- Glue together and re-sand, keeping all edges sharp.
- Stain or paint.
- Apply a clear top coat.
- Add the movement and hands.

MOVEMENT, HANDS: ARMOR CRAFTS

No.	Name	Size	Req'd
1	Front	1/2" x 3 1/2" – 21"	1
2	Side	1/2" x 1 3/4" – 21"	2
3	Back pine	1/4" x 3" – 21"	1
4	Top/bottom	1/2" x 1 1/4" – 2 1/2"	2
5	Quartz movement*	16" pend. lg.	1
6	Hands		1 pr.

Clock parts from Armor Crafts:
Movement – No. 22310
Hands – No. 805 or equal - 1 3/4" lg.

*2 3/4" dia. pend.

21"

16" pend.

2 3/4" dia.

FRONT VIEW

3 1/2"

SIDE VIEW

2"

Rabbet 1/4" wide
x 1/4" deep

Rabbet 1/2"
wide x
1/4" deep

10 1/2"

1"

3/8"

3/8"

1"

EXPLODED VIEW

5/16" dia. hole

2¹/₂"

1¹/₂"

3¹/₂"

1/2" dia. hole

7/8"

CUT OUT

3/8" 2¹/₄" 3/8"

Rabbet ¹/₄" wide
x ¹/₄" deep

¹/₄"

1

21"

2

3

Rabbet ¹/₂"
wide x
¹/₄" deep

¹/₄"

1/2"

CUT
OUT

3/8' 1" 3/8'

10¹/₂"

1"

FRONT VIEW

3¹/₂"

FRONT VIEW

1³/₄"

FRONT VIEW

3"

FIT-UP: TURNCRAFT CLOCKS

If you want a real challenge and an unusual project—here it is. You will amaze your family and friends and even yourself with this one. Use contrasting wood for each piece. Maple and walnut were used here.

Mat'l thickness

Slightly less than
material thickness

Position all 12
toward center

Center

LOOP
1 req'd

Enlarge 130%

Special instructions

- Cut all pieces to overall size according to the cutting list.
- Use a photocopier to enlarge the pattern 130%.
- Carefully cut out all the pieces. Be sure all the slots are the same width as the thickness of wood.
- Dry fit all the pieces. This will take a little adjusting and fitting as you put it together.
- Line up "X" and "X" on the band loops (part No. 8). Glue the pattern to the wood and cut out two identical loops. Soak overnight in water and roll around a bending jig (part No. 9). Tape in place. Let dry for 48 hours.
- Glue bands (part No. 8) to the outside ring (part No. 5).
- Carefully assemble and apply light glue.
- Add fit up (part No. 10).

TIME RING
1 req'd

Locations of ②
do not glue

Cut as shown (re-glue after
12,② in loop

No.	Name	Size	Req'd
1	Tim ring	$^1/8"$ x $4^1/2"$ sq.	1
2	Loop	$^1/8"$ x $2^1/4" - 2^5/8"$	12
3	Center	$^1/8"$ x $1^3/4"$ sq.	1
4	Pin	$^3/16"$ dia. $- ^5/8"$	1
5	Outside ring	$^1/8"$ x $6^3/4"$ sq.	1
6	Support	$^1/8"$ x $2^3/4"$ sq.	1
7	Back board	$^1/8"$ x $5^1/2"$ sq.	1
8	Band loop	$^1/8"$ x $^9/16" - 18^5/8"$	2
9	Bending jig	$^3/4"$ x $5^1/4"$ dia.	1
10	Miniature fit-up	$1^7/16"$	1

Fit-up from Turncraft Clocks Inc.:
No. 5517 - black and gold

$^1/4"$ dia.

$^1/2"$ dia.

BACK BOARD
1 req'd

Mat'l thickness

BENDING JIG FOR ⑧
1 req'd - $^3/4"$ tk.

Enlarge 130%

Mat'l thickness

$1^5/16"$ dia. or
to suit

SUPPORT
1 req'd

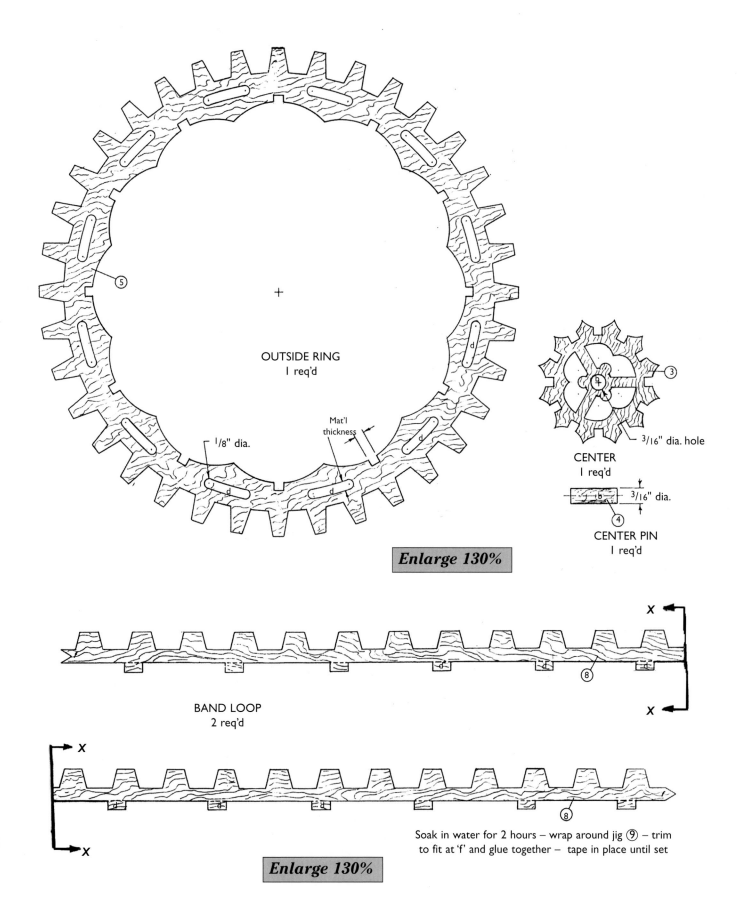

OUTSIDE RING
1 req'd

1/8" dia.

Mat'l
thickness

Enlarge 130%

CENTER
1 req'd

3/16" dia. hole

3/16" dia.

CENTER PIN
1 req'd

BAND LOOP
2 req'd

Soak in water for 2 hours — wrap around jig ⑨ — trim
to fit at 'f' and glue together — tape in place until set

Enlarge 130%

MOVEMENT, HANDS, BARS: PRECISION MOVEMENTS

This is large clock, but simple to make. It really looks great in an office or den. This model can be stained or painted. Oak or ash is a good choice if you plan to stain the finished clock. The clock pictured here was made of ash and painted black.

4" radius

1/8" radius

1/8" radius

8³/₄"

³/₄" dia.

④

10" dia.

3"

⑥

⑤

②

④

⑤

③

7" dia.

6³/₄" dia.

②

24"

⑦

③

⑧

⑤

1/8"

3/8"

④

Light gray

Rabbet
1/4" wide
3/8" deep

①

3"

3"

15¹/₄"

11¹/₄" drop

Dark gray

③/₄"

⁷/₈"

①

2³/₄" dia.

4" radius

8"

3/4"

FRONT VIEW

SIDE VIEW

EXPLODED VIEW

No.	Name	Size	Req'd
1	Base	3/4" x 8" – 24" long	1
2	Outer ring	3/4" x 10" dia.	1
3	Inner ring	1/8" x 7 3/8" dia.	1
4	Spacer	3/4" dia. x 7/8" long	4
5	Screw - fl. hd.	No. 8 – 2" long	4
6	Bars/dashes	3/4" long	1 set
7	Movement	12" pendulum lg.	1
8	Hands	3 3/8" length	1 pr.
9	Sawtooth hanger	To suit	1

Clock parts from Precision Movements:
Bars – No. 1022477 - 3/4" long
Movement – No. 1003274
Hands – No. 1008484

Special instructions

- Layout and cut out the base (part No. 1). Using a 1/8–inch radius with follower, make cut around the outside edge.
- Layout and cut out the outer ring (part No. 2).
- Layout and cut out the inner ring (part No. 3) using a 1/8-inch-radius router bit.
- Make the outer ring.
- Sand all the pieces.
- Check the thickness of your clock movement (part No. 7). The spacers (part No. 4) can be lengthened if movement is too thick. (A 7/8-inch-long spacer is shown).
- Stain or paint all pieces.
- Apply a clear top coat.
- Add dashes (part No. 6).
- Assemble all the pieces.
- Add the movement and hands.

I found an antique clock just like this one in a church basement. I liked it, so I took photos and designed a replica for this book. Oak or ash is a good choice for this clock. Wes and Alice used red oak.

FRONT VIEW

9 1/2"

15 1/2"

SIDE VIEW

2 1/2"

8¹/₂"

4¹/₂"

3" dia.

CUT OUT

10⁷/₁₆"

13¹/₂"

9"

①

FRONT VIEW

⑫

1⁷/₈"

3"

FRONT VIEW

A

FRONT VIEW

9"

9"

15

16

17

16

15

**VIEW
at A-A**

3/8"

1/8"

1/4"

3/4"

15

Chamfer
1/16" x 45°

3/8"

SECTION VIEW

FRONT VIEW

1 1/2"

1 1/8"

7

1"

1/8"   1/8"

3/4"

1/2"

1/4"

BOTTOM VIEW

FRONT VIEW

3/4"

8

1"

1/4"   1/8"

1/4"

1/2"

BOTTOM VIEW

FRONT VIEW

1 1/8"

3 1/4"

FRONT VIEW

1 1/8"

3 1/4"

Rabbet 1/4" wide x 1/4" deep in sides No. 2 as shown

1 1/2"

3/4"

4 1/2"

Notch for hinge

Notch for back

EXPLODED VIEW

No.	Name	Size	Req'd
1	Back	1/4" x 9" – 13 1/2"	1
2	Side	1/2" x 2" – 10 1/4"	2
3	Dial support	1/2" x 1 1/8" – 8"	2
4	Front	1/4" x 1 1/4" – 9"	1
5	Bottom board	3/16" x 2 1/2" – 9 1/2"	1
6	Top board	3/16" x 2 1/2" – 9 1/2"	1
7	Center tower	1/2" x 1" – 1 1/2"	1
8	Side tower	1/2" x 1" – 3/4"	1
9	Splat	1/4" x 1 1/8" – 3 1/4"	2
10	Side splat	1/4" x 1 1/8" – 1 7/8"	2
11	Cap	3/16" x 3/4" – 1 1/4"	3
12	Trim	1/2" x 1 7/8" – 3"	1
13	Dial - metal	Klockit #26087 (L)	1
14	Screw - rd. hd.	No. 4 – 3/8" long	4
15	Door	3/8" x 3/4" – 9"	4
16	Glass	8" x 8"	1
17	Glass support	1/8" x 3/16" – 36"	1
18	Hinge brass	3/4" x 3/4"	2
19	Hook/eye	Small	1

Clock parts from Klockit:
Quartz movement – No. 10043;
Hands – No. 66927

Special instructions

- Cut all pieces to overall size and sand all over.
- Layout parts No. 1, 9, 10 and 12, or simply bring this book to a copy center and have these pieces enlarged to the given dimensions.
- Cut out all the pieces.
- Make a simple box of parts No. 2, 3, 4 and 5. Don't forget to make notches for the hinges.
- Make a frame of parts No. 15, 16 and 17. (You might want to use small brads at the corners.)
- Make all the other pieces.
- Sand all over.
- Dry fit all pieces and trim if necessary.
- Assemble all the pieces.
- Stain and finish to suit.
- Add the dial face, movement and hands.

Special instructions
- Cut all wood to overall size and sand all over.
- Study the exploded view to see exactly how the clock is put together.
- Make the required rabbet cuts as shown.
- Cut out a 7^1/$_2$-inch-diameter hole for the dial face and an oval-shaped hole.
- Round the edges of the round and oval holes in the door. Rabbet a lip to support the glass.
- Make a box using parts No. 1, 3 and 4.
- Add supports (part No. 7).
- Fit the door to the box and sand all the pieces.
- To make a pattern for part No. 5, simply have an enlarged copy made that is 10^1/$_2$ inches wide.
- Dry fit all the remaining pieces and assemble the clock.
- Apply stain and top coat.
- Add the dial face and movement. (If using a paper dial face, glue it to the backing, part No. 8.)

MOVEMENT, HANDS: AMERICAN CLOCKMAKER; DIAL FACE: SHIPLEY CO.

No.	Name	Size	Req'd
1	Side	5/8" x 3^3/$_4$" – 28^1/$_2$"	2
2	Door	5/8" x 9^1/$_2$" – 28^7/$_{16}$"	1
3	Back	1/4" x 8^3/$_4$" – 28^1/$_2$"	1
4	Top/bottom	3/8" x 4^1/$_2$" – 11"	2
5	Splat	3/8" x 2^3/$_4$" – 10^1/$_2$"	1
6	Brace	1/2" x 1" – 2"	2
7	Support	1/2" x 2^1/$_2$" – 12^1/$_2$"	2
8	Backing	1/4" x 8^1/$_2$" – 8^1/$_2$"	1
9	Dial - paper	7" time ring	1
10	Glass	8" diameter	1
11	Movement w/ pend	20^1/$_4$" pendulum	1
12	Hands	3^1/$_2$" size	1 pr
13	Hinge	1^1/$_4$" x 1"	1 pr.
14	Screws	To suit	As req'd
15	Brads	7/8" long	As req'd
16	Glass - oval	2" x 3"	As req'd
17	Screw - rd. hd.	#4 - 3/4" lg.	4
18	Latch	Brass	1

Clock parts from The American Clockmaker:
Movement – No. 2306-G45
Hands – No. 2428
Dial face from Shipley Company: No. R-700

The original of this clock was made in 1820 by Aaron Willard, Jr., of Boston, Massachusetts. Choose an interesting wood. The original was made of cherry and had a beautiful, aged patina. I used figured maple wood for the clock shown here.

10½"

2¾"

5¼"

3⁄8"

13

10

7½" dia. hole

7

18

7

½"   6"   ½"

1

28½"

20¼"

5⁄8"

3

1

2

5⁄8"

1

9½"

2

13

16

3"

1 3⁄8"

4

11"

FRONT VIEW

5

6

4

9

8

10

11

7

2½"

3

30°

2

3¾"

¼"

4 1⁄16"

16

Pendulum

4

4½"

SIDE VIEW

Rabbet ¼" wide x
¼" deep

hands not shown

Notch for hinge 4" up
(down) from ends of ①

ASSEMBLY VIEW

CLOCK CASE: KLOCKIT CO.

Everyone loves a cuckoo clock. Until recently, I found it was impossible to make a cuckoo clock. Now with the help of the Klockit Company's complete movement, it is possible. This clock is very impressive. If you have a scroll saw, it is actually very easy to make. Mahogany was used for this clock.

Chain and weight
not shown

ASSEMBLY VIEW

Special instructions

Special instructions:
• Cut all the pieces to size according to
  the cutting list.
• Purchase and get a movement before
  starting. Be sure to check the opening in part No. 2 and width of parts 3
  and 4. Check that the face, part No. 5
  fits correctly. (These pieces need to
  be fit to the movement as you proceed.)
• Use a photocopier to enlarge the pattern to 165%.
• Glue the pattern to the wood and cut
  out all the pieces. Fit the pieces to
  each other and to the movement
  itself as you go.
• Sand all over and stain to suit.
• Fit and glue all the pieces together.
• Apply a light clear top coat spray.

Line up roof as shown →

② Back board
³/₁₆" thick

Fit clock case

31/32" dia. hole
8 places

FRONT VIEW

Enlarge 165%

Left side
3/16" thick

Fit to case

Fit to case

Cut at 30°

EDGE VIEW

30°

EDGE VIEW

30°

Right side
3/16" thick

Fit to case

Fit to case

Cut at 30°

Enlarge 165%

Check width of case

Fit up to roof

⑤ Face
³/16" thick

① ①

④ ③

¹/32" dia. hole
6 places

FRONT VIEW

Enlarge 165%

No.	Name	Size	Req'd
1	Clock case	Klockit No. 13061	1
2	Back board	³/16" x 8" – 12³/4"	1
3	Right side	³/16" x 4³/3" – 8¹/4"	1
4	Left side	³/16" x 4³/4" – 8¹/4"	1
5	Face	³/16" x 7¹/8" – 9¹/4"	1
6	Roof trim	³/16" x 11" – 8"	1
7	Tack (w/ head)	³/8" long	22
Clock parts from Klockit			

Roof trim
³/16" thick

³/32" dia. hole
14 places

¹/32" dia. hole
8 places

FRONT VIEW

Enlarge 165%

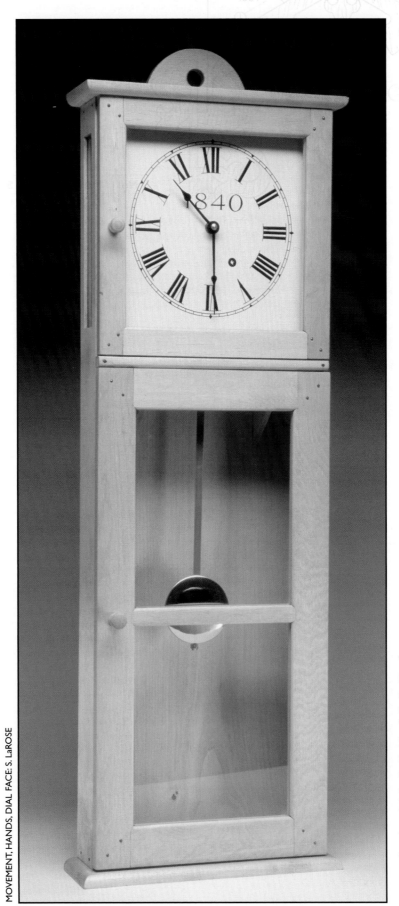

MOVEMENT, HANDS, DIAL FACE: S. LaROSE

This is one of my favorite clocks. The outer case is an exact copy of the original. The interior has been modified to accept a new movement. The original clock was designed and made by Isaac N. Youngs in 1840. This clock should be made of either pine or cherry.

2¼" radius   ⑥   ¾" dia. hole

④

⑬

⑳

⑫

㉕

⑦

⑧

31"

①

⑭

⑯

⑳

⑱

③

⑮

①

⑱

②

⑨

⑮

1840

⑰   ㉓

7¾"

¾"

2"

½"

1⅛"

7¾"
10"
door

1⅛"

½"

1⅝"

7¾"

19½"
door

¾"

7¾"

1⅝"

½"

⑲

⑪

⑫

⑭

①

⑲

15½"
pend.

1⅝"   6¾"   1⅝"
10"

11⅛"

FRONT VIEW

⑥

④   ⑤

⑩
⑪   ㉑

⑫

㉕
⑦
⑨

⑭

③

⑤

④

1¼"

7½"

1¼"
⅝"   ⅝"

①

½"   3"   ¼"

3⁹⁄₁₆"

SIDE VIEW

㉒

Rabbet ¼" wide x¼"deep
top, bottom, back edge

1/8"

1/2"

END VIEW

2 1/2"

5/8"   1 1/4"   5/8"

1 1/4"   1 1/8"

                         1"

7 1/2"   5 3/4"

                         1"

Route for glass
¼" wide x ³/8"deep
(4 sides)

                         3 1/4"

                         1"

30"

Inside
surface

7 3/4"

                         1"

                         1 5/8"

FRONT VIEW

No.	Name	Size	Req'd
1	Side	½" x 2½" – 30" lg.	2
2	Insert	¼" x 2¼" – 9½" lg.	2
3	Back	¼" x 9½" – 30" lg.	1
4	Top/Bottom	½" x 3⁹/₁₆" – 11⅛" lg.	2
5	Nail - sq. cut	¾" long (finish)	36
6	Hanger	½" x 2½" – 4½" lg.	1
7	Divider	½" x ½" – 10" lg.	1
8	Nail - sq. cut	1" long (finish)	2
9	Dial support	¼" x 1¾" – 13" lg.	2
10	Dial board	¼" x 8⅞" square	1
11	Dial face (7 dia.)	No. 133-871	1
12	Stile - upper	½" x 1⅛" – 10" lg.	2
13	Rail - upper	½" x 1⅛" – 9½" lg.	2
14	Stile - lower	½" x 1⅝" – 19½" lg.	2
15	Rail - lower	½" x 1⅝" – 9" lg.	2
16	Rail - center	½" x ¾" – 8" lg.	1
17	Glass - upper	3/32" x 8³/₁₆" sq.	1
18	Glass - lower	3/32" x 7³/₁₆" – 8³/₁₆"	2
19	Hinge (brass)	1" x 1"	4
20	Pull	9/16" dia. x 1¼" lg.	2
21	Glass - side	3/32" x 1⅝" – 7⅜"	2
22	Movement(15½)	No. 812076	1
23	Hands, black	No. 816013	1 pr.
24	Magnetic catch	⅜" dia.	2
	Dial face support	¼" x ¼" – 8⅞"	1

Clock parts from S. LaRose Inc.

Special instructions

- Study all the drawings very carefully. Be sure you fully understand how the various parts are made and put together before starting.
- Cut all the pieces to overall size and sand all over.
- Make all the pieces according to the detailed drawings. (Be sure to make a right-hand and left-hand pair of sides, part No. 1.)
- Assemble the case according to the exploded view. Fit the pieces together as you go.
- Sand all over.
- Apply a light stain and satin finish top coat.
- Glue the paper dial to the dial board (part No. 10). (You might want to add the 1840 date to the dial face.)
- Attach the movement and hands to the dial face.
- Add the movement to the clock case.

END VIEW

3/16"

1/2"

3/16"

⑫

1 1/8"

1"

1/8" radius

3/16"

TOP VIEW

3/16"

⑬

9 1/2"

1 1/2"

1"

45°

1 1/8"

END VIEW

3/4"

8"

3/4"

FRONT VIEW

Top door

10"

8"

45°

1"

1"

FRONT VIEW

3/16"

1/2"

3/16"

END VIEW

⑭

1 5/8"

1 1/2"

1 1/2"

45°

8"

19 1/2"

1/2"

9/16"

8"

45°

1 1/2"

FRONT VIEW

3/16"

3/16"

TOP VIEW

⑮

9"

1 5/8"

45°

1"

7"

1"

45°

1/2"

FRONT VIEW

8"

7"

1/2"

45°

⑯

1/2"

45°

3/4"

FRONT VIEW

⑤

⑫ ⑭

⑬ ⑮

⑯

EXPLODED VIEW

$3^5/16$" $4^1/2$" $3^5/16$"

Notch only one piece (top)

$1/4$"

$3^9/16$"

TOP VIEW

④

$11^1/8$"

$5/8$"

FRONT VIEW

$1/2$" radius - 3 edges only

$3/4$" dia. hole

$2^1/4$" radius

$1/2$"

⑥

$2^1/2$"

$1/2$"

$1^3/8$"

$1/4$"

$4^1/2$"

FRONT VIEW

END VIEW

'Round' front

$1/2$"

END VIEW

$1/2$"

⑨

13"

$1^1/2$"

$1^3/4$"

SIDE VIEW

10"

⑦

FRONT VIEW

$9/16$" dia.

$3/16$" dia.

$7/16$" dia.

$1/4$" dia.

$5/32$"

$7/16$"

$3/32$"

$9/16$"

$1^1/4$"

SIDE VIEW

Putty glass in place ⑰⑱ &㉑

EXPLODED VIEW

Special instructions

- Study all the drawings very carefully. Be sure you fully understand how the various parts are made and put together before starting.
- The front and side molding (parts No. 12 and 13) are the most difficult pieces to make. Use a piece of wood $1/2$" x $1^5/8$" x 15" and a router bit with a follower.
- Make the large case pieces (parts No. 2, 3, 5, 10 and 11).
- Assemble the case, keeping everything square.
- Make the door according to the detail drawing and fit it to the case assembly.
- Make and add the remaining pieces.
- Make the molding pieces (parts No. 12 and 13) using a router with a follower. Cut the molding from a piece $1/2$" x $1^5/8$" 15". After routing, make the $7/16$-inch-wide cut and then cut it into three pieces, as shown.
- With a lathe, make parts No. 4, 19, 20 and 21. (If you don't have a lathe, find someone who does custom turning.) To make two identical, half-round pieces. make two pieces $9/32$" x $9/16$" x 16" inches long. Glue them together with a piece of paper between the two pieces. Let the glue set overnight. Turn the assembled piece according to the drawing, then separate the pieces along the paper with a knife or putty knife.
- Add the turnings.
- Sand all over.
- Apply stain and clear top coat.
- Add glass pieces (parts No. 22 and 23).
- Add the dial face, movement and hands. (Lyre optional.)

This is the most formal clock in the book. It is very elegant and should be hung in a formal setting. Be sure to use a beautiful wood with an interesting grain. Cherry was used here. To make the finials, you will need a lathe, or you can purchase very similar finials. You also might want to consider a brass mechanical movement in place of a quartz movement.

MOVEMENT, HANDS, LYRE: STEEBAR CORP.

FRONT VIEW

7"

22"

SIDE VIEW

3³/₄"

1 1/8"

3/4"

2 1/14" r

2 13/16" r

①

3/16"

5/8"

15 3/8"

12 9/16"

14 1/4"

23

5/8"

5/16"

Gray
Putty

24

7/8" radi

*

+

+

INSIDE VIEW

3/4"

4 1/2"

3/4"

6"

TOP VIEW

④

1 5/16"

9/16" sq.

3/16"
3/16"

9/16" d.

1/2" d.

3/8" d.

14 1/4"

10 7/16"

3/16"
3/16"

1/2" d.

9/16" d.

1 11/16"

9/16" sq.

FRONT VIEW

2⁷/₈"   3/16" d.   7/16"

9/32"   3/4"   30°

3³/₁₆"   **END VIEW**

⑪   **FRONT VIEW**

Cut at approx. 20° as shown - fit with ⑪

7/16"

⑩   Saw kerf approx. 1/4" apart

6³/₈"

FRONT VIEW

Fit at assembly   ⑩

⑪   **AS BENT**   ⑪

2¹³/₁₆" r

TOP VIEW

3/16" dia. hole

3/4"

5/16"

7/8"   ⑮

15/16"

FRONT VIEW

3¹/₄" r

⑯

1¹/₈"

7/8"

FRONT VIEW

3/16" dia. hole

⑰

TOP VIEW

1/8"

3/8"   **FRONT VIEW**   ⑥   1/4" r

4¹/₂"

3/16" dia. hole

5/8"

3/8"

1³/₈"   ⑱

FRONT VIEW

2¹/₂"

BOTTOM VIEW

45°

9

1³/₁₆"

2¹/₈"

1" dia.

5³/₄"

SIDE VIEW

3/16"

1¹³/₁₆"

END VIEW

3/8"

FRONT VIEW

3³/₄"

7

3/16"

1/8" r

3/16"

5/8"

2¹/₈"

BOTTOM VIEW

3/4"

FRONT VIEW

3/16"

9/32" r

8

3"

3/16" dia. hole

5/8"

1⁵/₈"

BOTTOM VIEW

7"

1/8"

7/16"

1/16"

FRONT VIEW

6¹/₄"

5

5/8"

25/32"

2²³/₃₂"

2²³/₃₂"

25/32"

2⁵/₁₆"

3¹¹/₁₆"

3/4"

BOTTOM VIEW

FRONT VIEW

1¹/₈"

9/16"

2¹³/₁₆" r

3" dia.

⑨

CUT OUT

⑨

3¹/₂"

15³/₈"

12⁹/₁₆"

14¹/₄"

③

5⁵/₈"

TOP VIEW

②

3/16" 3/8"

1/4"

INSIDE VIEW

1¹¹/₁₆"

9/16" r

CUT OUT

1/8" 1/8"

1³/₈"

10⁹/₁₆"

14¹/₄"

9/16" r

1⁵/₈"

2"

2⁹/₁₆"

1/2"

7/16"

Cut to fit

4"

(13)

(13)

45°

45°

(12)

7"

2 13/16" r

(12)

Notch for (16)

90°

As folded
cut to fit
at assembled

(13)

(13)

(13)

4"

Cut to fit

1 5/8"

1/2"

3/16"d. 9/16"d. 5/16"d. 7/16"d. 1/4"d. 9/16"d. 1 1/8"d. 3/16"d. 5/16"d. 3/32"d. 7/16"d.

(19)

1/4" 9/32" 1/8" 5/32" 5/32" 11/16" 11/32" 3/16"

1/16" 3/32" 1/16"

2 7/16"

SIDE VIEW

3/16"d. 7/8"d. 1/2"d. 1"d. 3/8"d. 9/16"d. 3/32"d. 3/16"d.

(20)

1/4" 1/4" 7/16" 5/8" 9/32" 7/32"

1/16" 1/16"

2 3/16"

SIDE VIEW

(4)

Paper (glue between wood)

No.	Name	Size	Req'd
1	Front	$5/8" \times 6" - 15^3/8"$	1
2	Side	$3/8" \times 2^9/16" - 14^1/4"$	2
3	Back (pine)	$1/4" \times 5^5/8" - 15^3/8"$	1
4	Column (split)	$9/32" \times 9/16" - 14^1/4"$	2
5	Bottom	$7/16" \times 3^{11}/16" - 7"$	1
6	Bottom	$3/8" \times 2^1/2" - 4^1/2"$	1
7	Bottom	$3/8" \times 2^1/8" - 3^3/4"$	1
8	Bottom	$3/4" \times 1^5/8" - 3"$	1
9	Dial support	$3/16" \times 1^{13}/16" - 5^3/4"$	2
10	Top - center	$7/16" \times 3^3/16" - 6^1/2"$	1
11	Top - side	$7/16" \times 3^3/16" - 3/4"$	2
12	Front molding	$7/16" \times 1/2" - 15"$	1
13	Side molding	Made from (12)	2
14	Pin - bottom	$3/16"$ dia. $\times 1^9/16"$	1
15	Base	$3/4" \times 7/8" - 15/16"$	1
16	Front trim	$1/8" \times 7/8" - 1^1/8"$	1
17	Top	$1/8" \times 1^1/8" - 1^1/8"$	1
18	Side trim	$1/8" \times 3/8" - 1^3/8"$	2
19	Top finial	$1^1/8"$ dia. $\times 3^7/16"$	3
20	Bottom finial	$1"$ dia. $\times 3^3/16"$	1
21	Side finial	$11/16"$ dia. $\times 3^7/16"$	2
22	Side glass*	$1^5/8" \times 12"$	2
23	Front glass*	$5" \times 14^5/8"$	1
24	Putty	To suit	
25	Dial - metal		1
26	Quartz movement	$11^1/2"$ pendulum lg.	1
27	Hands		1pr.
28	Brass hanger	To suit	1

Clock parts from Steebar Corp.
Movement – No. WCP-250-S with chimes
Hands – No. 12
Dial – No. 115MM ($4^1/2"$ dia.)
Lyre (optional) No. Lyre-4

Not shown:
25, 26, 27, 28

ASSEMBLY VIEW

SIDE VIEW

Everyone is attracted to a tall case clock, known as a grandfather clock. These add beauty, warmth, charm and substance to any room. Through the years, the grandfather clock has been a hallmark stating that its owner has achieved a certain level of success. A tall case clock is very special woodworking project that will likely be passed on to your children and grandchildren. A handmade grandfather clock is truly a prized possession.

Today, the price of an antique version of this clock is extremely prohibitive. The original of this particular model, made by Eli Terry in 1802, at Plymouth, Connecticut, would probably cost well over $10,000—if it could be purchased. It had a one-day wooden movement with a printed paper dial. A good reproduction would cost well over $1,500 and would most likely have a plywood or pressed-wood back. The original clock is kept in a clock museum in Bristol, Connecticut. It was made of pine. A painted grain pattern was added to it to make it look as if the clock were made from an expensive hardwood.

The dial for this clock can be purchased from any one of the suppliers listed in the Appendix, but it is not difficult to make your own out of 1/4-inch-thick wood. Paint the wood an off-white and add a light wash around the edges for that "aged" look. Lay out the face with a drafter's technical pen.

The movement is supported on a shelf between the two side boards of the case. Two short boards, 5/8" x 1 1/2" x 6", secured to the case will hold the shelf that supports the movement and allow the weights to hang through the slot. The shelf is then simply set on the two boards attached to the side boards.

Attach the pendulum and weights. Adjust the "crotch" (the arm at the rear of the movement that is attached to the pendulum rod) so the pendulum will "tick" and "tock" at an equal distance from the center of the clock. Bend the crutch one way or the other if necessary. This is called "putting the clock into beat." The clock speed is adjusted by raising or lowering the pendulum (up to speed the clock up, down to slow it down). Test the clock for 24 hours or so before attaching the face, hands and hood to the clock.

MOVEMENT: S. LaROSE

Special instructions

- Study all drawings so that you fully understand how everything is made and assembled.
- Cut all the pieces to overall size per the parts list. The original was made of pine, but any nice hardwood would look better.
- Use a photocopier to enlarge the pattern 200%.
- As you make the individual pieces, dry fit each piece with its mating piece(s).
- Make up the basic body assembly using parts No. 1, 2 and 3. Be sure to keep everything square.
- Assemble the front panel using parts No. 4, 5 and 44.
- Carefully finish up the body assembly (refer to the exploded view). Fit pieces as you proceed.
- Fit the hood assembly to the body. Be sure the bottom moldings (parts No. 25 and 26) easily slide over the molding on the body (parts No. 12 and 13).
- Complete the hood assembly and the

door. (Refer to the exploded view.)
- Make up the dial face.
- If you are using a quartz movement, attach it to the dial and add the hands. (If you are using a brass mechanical movement, you will have to add a shelf to support the dial. Cut a shelf to fit your movement. Cut a slot for the pendulum and a notch for the weights. Position the shelf between the two side panels (part No. 1) so the center shaft of the movement lines up with the center hole of the dial face.
- Screw the dial face to the sides (part No. 1).
- Remove the dial face and the movement.
- Sand the case and the hood and wipe the piece clean.
- Apply a stain to suit and three top coats of clear satin finish. (Sand between each coat
- Re-install the movement, weights, pendulum, dial face and hands.

3/4"

2

3/8"   3/8"

9⁵/₁₆"   3/4"   6"

Notch backboard
3/8" in from sides

2

1

13¹/₄"

1

1

82¹/₁₆"

72³/₄"

1

1

2

3/4"   3   3/4"

59¹/₂"

3

3

BASIC BODY ASSEMBLY

12"   6³/₄"

FRONT PANEL ASSEMBLY

No.	Name	Size	Req'd
1	Side	$3/4" \times 6^{3/4}" - 72^{3/4}"$	2
2	Back (pine)	$2/4" \times 12" - 82^{1/16}"$	1
3	Bottom (pine)	$3/4" \times 6" - 10^{1/2}"$ lg.	1
4	Style	$3/4" \times 3^{3/4}" - 59^{1/2}"$ lg.	2
5	Rail	$3/4" \times 7^{1/2}" - 5^{3/4}"$ lg.	3
6	Side spacer (pine)	$7/8" \times 7^{1/2}" - 3"$ lg.	4
7	Front spacer	$7/8" \times 13^{3/4}" - 3"$ lg.	2
8	Side skirt	$3/4" \times 8^{7/8}" - 18"$ lg.	2
9	Front skirt	$3/4" \times 15^{1/4}" - 18"$ lg.	1
10	Door	$3/4" \times 5" - 32^{1/4}"$ lg.	1
11	Hinge (brass)	To suit (1" lg.)	2
12	Top side molding	$1" \times 2" - 8^{1/2}"$ lg.	2
13	Top front molding	$1" \times 2" - 14"$ lg.	1
14	Center side molding	$1" \times 2" - 9"$ lg.	2
15	Center. front molding	$1" \times 2" - 15"$ lg.	1
16	Leg support	$3/4" \times 2^{5/8}" -$ to fit	1
17	Back leg	$1^{1/2}" \times 2^{5/8}" - 3^{1/2}"$ lg.	2
18	Front/side legs	$1^{1/2}" \times 2^{5/8}" - 3^{1/2}"$ lg.	4
19	Screws - flat head	#8 - 2" lg.	12
20	Bottom side molding	$1" \times 1^{3/4}" - 10^{1/8}"$ lg.	2
21	Btm front molding	$1" \times 1^{3/4}" - 17^{1/4}"$ lg.	1
22	Filler	$1/4" \times 5/8" - 30"$ lg.	2
23	Side	$3/4" \times 7^{1/2}" - 21^{3/4}"$ lg.	2
24	Trim	$3/4" \times 3^{1/4}" - 13^{5/8}"$ lg.	1
25	Base - front	$1" \times 1^{1/2}" - 15^{1/16}"$ lg.	1
26	Base - side	$1" \times 1^{1/2}" - 9"$ lg.	2
27	Screws - flat head	No. 6 - 2" lg.	6
28	Top board	$3/4" \times 10^{3/4}" - 18^{1/2}"$ lg.	1
29	Front dentil	$1/2" \times 3" - 14^{5/8}"$ lg.	1
30	Side dentil	$1/2" \times 3" - 8^{3/8}"$ lg.	2
31	Top front molding	$1" \times 2" - 16^{5/8}"$ lg.	1
32	Top side molding	$1" \times 2" - 9^{3/4}"$ lg.	2
33	Stile	$3/4" \times 1^{5/16}" - 18^{7/16}"$ lg.	2
34	Bottom rail	$3/4" \times 1^{5/16}" - 13^{11/16}"$ lg.	1
35	Top rail	$3/4" \times 6^{3/16}" - 3^{11/16}"$ lg.	1
36	Brass pull	$3/8"$ dia.	2
37	Glass	To fit	1
38	Hinge - brass	$7/8" -$ to fit	2
39	Putty - black	As req'd	
40	Platform	$3/4" \times 5^{1/4}" - 10^{1/2}"$ lg.	1
41	Dial face	$3/4" \times 11^{3/4}" - 17^{1/2}"$ lg.	1
42	Movement	To suit	1
43	Hands	To suit	1 pr.
44	Peg (optional)	$1/4"$ dia. $\times 3/4"$ lg.	18

Movement from S. Larose, Inc.:
No. 084069 with 42" pendulum and simple bell strike

12"

14"

3/4"

1"

2"

8 1/2"

② 13

1/8" r

5/16"

② 4

2 1/4"

1"

11

②

⑩ 1

1" × 1" × 45°
brace

1 30 1/2"
door

4

DOOR EDGE

7 1/2"

Bead

5"

11

⑩

1"

3 1/4"

15

14 15

3/4"

1 3/8"

1 1/2"

14

18"

15 1/4"

9 1/8"

20
21

1 3/4"

Bead

2 5/8"

16

21

20

1"

BODY ASSEMBLY

Important: Overall M
this level must be 8

Pegs (optional)

Notch at slight angle

EXPLODED VIEW OF BODY

28

18¹/₂"

28

3/4"

24

2¹/₄"

1"

23

18¹/₂"

13⁵/₈"

25

1"

1¹/₂"

¹/₄"

Fit over moldings 12 & 13 on body

14¹/₁₆"

Fit hood assembly to body

HOOD ASSEMBLY

10³/₄"

28

24

8¹/₄"

7¹/₂"

23

Notch for hinge

23¹/₂"

26

8⁹/₃₂"

8¹/₈"

25

26

1"

9/16"

¹/₄"

1"

¹/₂"

1¹/₂"

$^{3}/_{16}$" dia. bead

33

37

VIEW AT A-A

A

35

A

33

33

$5^{1}/_{4}$" r

$6^{3}/_{16}$"

$1^{1}/_{4}$"

33

$1/_{12}$"

$^{1}/_{8}$" dia. hole

$18^{7}/_{16}$"

$12^{1}/_{4}$"

$6^{7}/_{8}$"

34

$1^{5}/_{16}$"

$11^{1}/_{16}$"

$1^{5}/_{16}$"

$^{3}/_{4}$"

$13^{11}/_{16}$"

DOOR ASSEMBLY

HOOD ASSEMBLY

DENTIL DETAIL

Shelf for mechanical
movement to suit

Position so center
shaft is located at
center of dial time ring

(2) $^5/8$" x $1^1/2$" – 6"

**SUGGESTED MOVEMENT
SUPPORT DETAIL**

$3^5/8$"

EXPLODED VIEW OF HOOD

41

5³/₄" R

13¹/₂"

10" dia. time ring

1⁵/₈"

17¹/₂"

7³/₄"

Prime and
paint white

6"

6"

12"

1¹/₂"

3¹/₂"

18

2⁵/₈"

Cut as shown

LEG DETAIL

Enlarge 200%

½" squares

Off white

60

55

5

50

10

45

15

¾/8"

Ferry

½" diameter

1⅛"

40

20

Locate from
movement

35

25

30

17½"

11¾"

CLOCK MUSEUMS (USA)

This list includes museums that have a substantial collection of clocks, watches, or both.

To fully enjoy and study original clocks, I recommend you visit one or more of the following museums. In seeing original antique clocks, you will have a feel of clocks made years ago and a better understanding of the clock you want to create now.

American Clock and Watch Museum
100 Maple Street
Bristol, CT 06010
(203) 583-6070
http://www.nawcc.org

Bily Clock Exhibit Horology Museum
Spillville, IA 52168
(319) 562-3569

Henry Ford Museum
Greenfield Village
Dearborne, MI 48100
(313) 271-1620

Henry Francis DuPont
Winterthur Museum
Winterthur, DE 19735
(302) 656-8591 or
(800) 448-3883

Hoffman Foundation
Newark Public Library
Newark, NY 14513
(315) 331-4370

Metropolitan Museum of Art
5th Avenue and 82nd Street
Manhattan, NY
(212) 535-7710

Museum of the American
Watchmakers Institute
3700 Harrison Avenue
Cincinnati, OH
(513) 661-3838

National Museum of Clocks and Watches
514 Poplar Street
Columbia, PA 17512
(717) 684-8261
http://www.nawcc.org

Old Clock Museum
929 East Preston
Pharr, TX 78577
(512) 787-1923

The Bily Brothers

Joseph was born at Calmar, Iowa, on September 5, 1880; his brother Frank was born on their home farm four miles north of Spillville on October 1, 1884. Their parents, John and Mary Andera Bily, were natives of Bohemia. The father arrived in this country at 14 years old It is from their mother that the brothers inherited their artistic talents.

By trade the Bily Brothers were farmers and carpenters; carving was just a hobby. Their father was opposed to their hobby and many times told them that they were wasting their time.

The two brothers divided their work; Joseph did the designing, drawing of the plans and joining of the woods; his younger brother, Frank, did nearly all of the carving and cutting. They also made all of their own installations and repairs.

Although their inspiration for carving was a natural talent from their very early childhood, the idea of carving clocks was derived from their Norwegian neighbor, who carved a clock but was unable to properly equip it with mechanism. He asked the brothers to install the works in the clock. This gave the brothers the idea to carve their own clocks, and in 1913, they began their most unique hobby.

Nearly all of the main clocks the brothers made have moveable mechanical figures and musical chimes. This mechanism is of the brothers' own construction. The clock works and chimes are factory-made, except for one hall clock which has carved wooden works. Most of their work is done in native wood, such as black or American walnut, butternut, hard maple and oak. Some imported woods, such as European cherry, mahogany, box wood and white holly, were also used.

Although they received various offers for their clocks, the brothers never accepted any of them. In 1947 they made arrangements for the entire clock collection to became the property of the town of Spillville after their death. The collection is never to be broken up in any way and always to remain in Spillville.

Old Salem, Inc.
614 Main Street
Winston-Salem, NC 27100
(919) 723-3688

Old Sturbridge Village
Sturbridge, MA 01566
(617) 347-3362

Smithsonian Institute
National Museum of American History
Washington, DC 20000
(202) 357-1300

The Time Museum
7801 E. State Street
Rockford, IL 61125-0285
(815) 398-6000

Willard House
Grafton, MA 01519
(617) 839-3500

PRODUCTS AND SERVICE

The following companies provide excellent products and service. Joyce and I have worked with all of them through the years and highly recommend them. (If by chance we have left out any company, it is only because we are not aware of them at this time.) Write and ask for their catalogs. Be sure to tell them Joyce and I sent you.

Interior view of The Time Museum, Rockford, Illinois. (Photo used with permission of The Time Museum.)

THE AMERICAN CLOCKMAKER
(Parts and kits)
PO Box 326
Clintonville, WI 54929
(800) 236-7300

ARMOR CRAFTS
WOODWORKERS SPECIALTIES
PO Box 445
East Northport, NY 11730
(800) 292-8296

BRADCO ENTERPRISES
31ST Street N
St. Petersburg, FL 33714
(727) 894-7176

CHERRY TREE TOYS
PO Box 369
Belmont, OH 43718
(800) 848-4363

KLOCKIT
PO Box 636
Lake Geneva, WI 53147
(800) 556-2548

KUEMPEL CHIME CLOCKWORKS AND
STUDIO (Clock kits, and large brass movements)
21195 Minnetonka Boulevard
Excelsior, MN 55331
(800) 328-6445

MERRITT'S ANTIQUES
1860 Weavertown Rd.
PO box 277
Douglassville, PA 19518
(800) 345-4101

NATIONAL ARTCRAFT CO.
7996 Darroll Road
Twinsburg, OH 44087
(888) 937-2723

PRECISION MOVEMENTS
PO Box 1269
N 3211 County Road H
Lake Geneva, WI 53147
(800) 533-2024

S. LaROSE, INC.
PO Box 21208
3223 Yanceyville Street
Greensboro, NC 27405
(336) 621-1936

SHIPLEY CO. (Clock, glass and dials)
2075 S. University Blvd. Suite #199
Denver, Co 80210
(303) 777-0714

STEEBAR CORP.
PO Box 463
Andover, NJ 07821
(973) 383-1026

TURNCRAFT CLOCKS, INC.
PO Box 100
Mound, MN 55364
(800) 544-1711

KIDDER MFG. CO., LTD.
39 Glen Cameron Road Unit #3
Thornhill, Ontario
Canada L3T 1P1
(800)-263-3556

CLOCK BOOK SUPPLIERS

Arlington Book Co.
2706 Elsmore Street
Fairfax, VA 22031-1409
Phone (703) 280-2005

U.S. Books
7707 Kiva Drive
Austin, TX 78749-2917
Phone (512) 892-4220

CHERRY TREE TOYS (Above)
Has an INSIDER'S CLUB you might want to
inquire about.

ANTIQUE SHOPS

A wonderful place to visit if you
are in the northeast is:

Delaney Antique Clocks
435 Main Street
West Townsend, Massachusetts
01474

They have one of the largest
selections of antique clocks for sale;
it is like visiting a museum. If you
appreciate old clocks, you will enjoy
this visit.

RECOMMENDED PAINT SUPPLIERS

For the clocks in this book that
require a painted finish and for a
very professional, unusual finish try
some of their unusual products:
Special Faux Finishing, Crackle
Finishes, Glazing and Stains.

DELTA TECHNICAL COATINGS, INC.
2550 Pellissier Place
Whittier, CA 90601
(800) 423-4135

VISIONS
7106 N. Alpine Road
Rockford, IL 61111
(800) 654-6114

CLOCK PLANS

Most of the companies listed in
the appendix provide many more
clock plans for you to choose.

This is a clock pattern I developed for Steebar Corp. They have many other clock patterns for you to choose. (Photo used by permission of Steebar Corp.)

APPENDIX B

CLOCK PROJECT WOOD

COMMON NAME	SCIENTIFIC NAME	DESCRIPTION
Afrormosia	*Pericopsis elata*	Exposure darkens the heartwood to a deep orange-brown. Straight to interlocked grain.
Avodire*	*Turraeanthus africanus*	Heartwood is creamy white to pale yellow and darkens to a golden yellow on exposure. Straight but sometimes wavy or interlocking grain.
Butternut	*Juglans cinerea*	Sapwood is white to light grayish-brown; heartwood is light brown, sometimes streaked with dark brown or red. Straight-grained.
Cherry, American	*Prunus serotina*	Sapwood is whitish to reddish-brown; heartwood varies from reddish brown to deep red or light reddish brown. Fine, straight grain.
Chestnut, American	*Castanea dentata*	Heartwood is pale brown with wide growth rings; occasionally "wormy" due to blight.
Cocobolo*	*Dalbergia retusa*	Heartwood color is deep red with yellow, orange, red and even purple streaks. Irregular grain.
Elm, red	*Ulmus hollandica*	Also known as Dutch elm or English elm. Hardwood is brown with distinct annual rings. Straight-grained.
Elm, American white	*Ulmus americana*	Hardwood is medium reddish-brown. Straight, sometimes interlocking grain.
Goncalo Alves*	*Astronium fraxinifolium*	Sapwood is brownish-white; heartwood golden brown to reddish brown with irregular blackish-brown streaks. Wavy or interlocked grain.
Lacewood	*Platanus hybrida*	Heartwood is light reddish-brown with a flecked appearance. Straight-grained.
Mahogany, African*	*Khaya ivorensis*	Heartwood is light to deep reddish-brown. Straight to interlocking grain. Many different varieties exist under the popular name mahogany.
Maple, Sugar or Hard	*Acer saccharum*	Wood is creamy-white with a reddish tinge; heartwood on large trees may be dark brown. Straight-grained.
Mapel, Soft	*Acer rubrum*	Creamy-white wood. Straight-grained, but highly figured when sliced.
Oak, American Red	*Quercus rubra*	Sapwood is whitish to grayish or pale reddish-brown; heartwood is pinkish to light reddish-brown. Straight-grained.
Oak, American White	*Quercus alba*	Color varies from pale yellow-brown to beige with a pinkish tint. Straight-grained.
Pine, Yellow	*Pinus strobus*	Heartwood color varies from a pale straw color to light reddish-brown. Straight-grained.
Poplar, Yellow (Tulip)	*Liriodendron tulipifera*	Sapwood is whitish; heartwood varies from pale yellowish-brown to pale olive brown with darker streaks. Straight-grained.
Purplewood*	*Peltogyne paniculata*	Sapwood is pale red or pink; heartwood darkens to purple upon exposure. Straight-grained.
Satinwood*	*Chlorxylon swietenia*	Heartwood is a golden yellow color, darkening to golden brown with darker streaks. Interlocked and variegated grain.
Walnut	*Juglans nigra*	Heartwood is rich, dark brown. Mostly straight-grained, occasionally wavy or curly.
Zebrawood*	*Microberlinia brazzavillensis*	Heartwood is light golden-yellow with streaks of dark brown or black. Interlocked or wavy grain.

*These woods may have toxic properties. Research them carefully before using them in a clock project.

Carving the Human Face - Capturing Character and Expression in Wood
By Jeff Phares

If you're having trouble creating life-like human faces, this is the book for you! World Champion carver Jeff Phares, well known for his lifelike busts and masks, reveals his techniques for creating masterful human portraits in wood.

- More than 350 instructional photographs to take you from a block of butternut to the finished facial mask of a Native American warrior.
- Diagrams explaining facial anatomy and how it relates to carving masks and busts.

Woodcarvers and sculptors alike will find new material and techniques inside this definitive, full-color guide.

$24.95
104 pages, 8.5x11, soft cover
ISBN# 1-56523-102-3

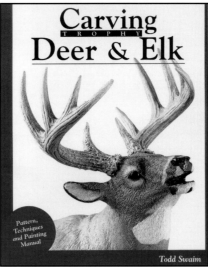

Carving Trophy Deer & Elk
By Todd Swaim

No one can capture the majesty of deer & elk like wildlife artist Todd Swaim.

- Complete step-by-step techniques shown in full color
- Beautiful gallery of finished examples
- Anatomy sketches, painting charts & hair tract illustrations

$19.95
74 pages, 8.5x11, soft cover
ISBN# 1-56523-089-2

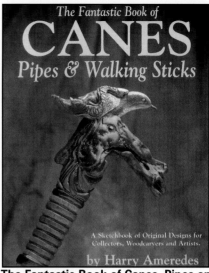

The Fantastic Book of Canes, Pipes and Walking Sticks
By Harry Ameredes

This sketchbook will keep you fascinated for hours!

- Original pen & ink design sketches
- Hundreds of ideas
- Highly recommended

$12.95
110 pages, 8x10, soft cover
ISBN# 1-56523-048-5

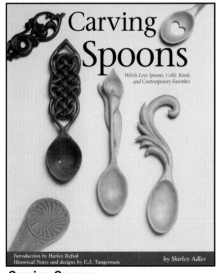

Carving Spoons
By Shirley Adler

Spoons are fun, simple projects to develop your carving creativity & express yourself.

- 23 full size ready-to-use patterns
- Full color step-by-step instructions
- Features Welsh love spoons & Celtic knots

$14.95
75 pages, 8.5x11, soft cover
ISBN# 1-56523-092-2

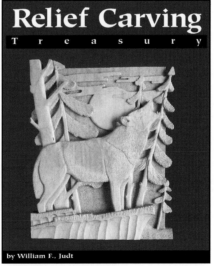

Relief Carving Treasury
By William F. Judt

Through pictures & patterns, see what is possible for the carver working in relief.

- 16 gorgeous projects (intermediate)
- Full color photographs
- Detailed notes & technique tips

$14.95
74 pages, 8.5x11, soft cover
ISBN# 1-56523-097-3

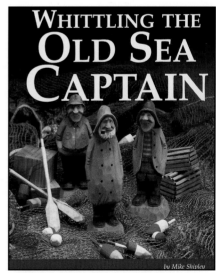

Whittling the Old Sea Captain
By Mike Shipley

Ahoy, there mate! Come aboard with carver Mike Shipley as he shows you how to carve a sea-worthy old captain and his crew.

- More than 100 step-by-step photos on carving, painting & staining
- Patterns for the Captain and his 1st & 2nd mates
- Information & more patterns for making buoys, lobster traps & wooden crates

$12.95
31 pages, 8.5x11, soft cover
ISBN# 1-56523-075-2

Carving
books make
great gifts!

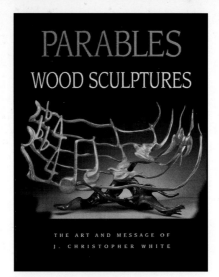

Parables: Wood Sculptures
By J. Christopher White

We're excited about publishing this book! Chris White
takes gnarled trees and roots and works within these
natural forms to create stunningly beautiful works of art.
These carved sculptures are sometimes realistic,
sometimes stylized, but always highly evocative—even
poetic and full of meaning.

The full color gallery photos and technical chapters
appeal to carvers, sculptors and fine artists. The sheer
beauty of each piece is accentuated with the artist's
description of its creation and how it relates to his deep
faith. This is an inspiring and interesting coffee table
book.

$34.95 *(Available in November 1999)*
128 pages, 8.5x11, hard cover
ISBN# 11-56523-122-8

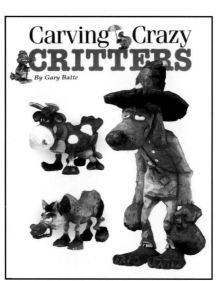

Carving Crazy Critters
By Gary Batte

Bring a smile to even the most somber face with the
characters in Gary Batte's new book. Ten clever projects
are featured, complete with patterns, and finishing
instructions. Sneak up on a down-and-out friend with "Al
E. Gater," delight the woman in your life with
"Buttercup, the Queen of Moo," give a hunter a laugh
with "Flea-Bitis," make a child laugh with "Grumpy
Gorilla," or move a slow-poke along with "Speedy the
Tortoise."

You'll enjoy carving these delightful pieces as much as
a friend or family member will enjoy receiving them.

$14.95
64 pages, 8.5x11, soft cover
ISBN# 1-56523-114-7

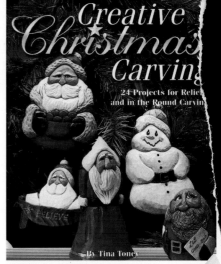

Creative Christmas Carving
By Tina Toney

Santas, santas, santas...and a couple of
snowmen too! Within the pages of this
book, you'll find 24 brilliant designs to
decorate a Christmas tree and fill your
home with the holiday spirit.

Patterns for each design are included, as
well as a step-by-step demonstration with
more than 50 photos to get you started.

Each ornament is carved from commer-
cially available turnings or 3/8" thick bass-
wood.

$14.95
64 pages, 8.5x11, soft cover.
ISBN# 1-56523-120-1

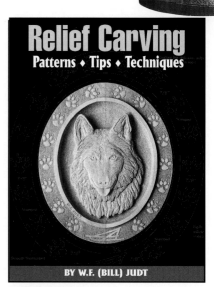

Relief Carving - Patterns, Tips & Techniques
By William F. Judt

Join the ever-growing cadre of relief carvers with this
complete introduction to relief carving. Author and
artist Bill Judt shares tricks of the trade and personal
insights gathered over his 13 years of relief carving.

Moving to the practical side of relief carving, he covers
everything from choosing woods and buying chisels to
laminating boards and stamping backgrounds. Included
are a step-by-step demonstration and ready-to-use patterns to help you start your own relief-carving venture.
Bill also includes advice for selling your work.

$19.95 *(Available in November 1999)*
120 pages, 8.5x11, soft cover
ISBN# 1-56523-124-4